What was the Question, Sir?

*To dear Theresa & Joe
my good neighbours
Best Wishes,
Alan.*

To Odhran and Aoibhinn

Foreword

"We must become the change we wish to see in the world,"
Mahatma Gandhi

Flan has lived out the mantra of this great man. If change has been required he has been the one to lead, showing courage and energy in tackling problems and in taking on new initiatives. He has done so with such enthusiasm and commitment that he has brought many others on board. His belief and trust in people has enabled them to take on tasks that they may have otherwise considered to be beyond them. He has earned huge respect in Thurles and far beyond it by his consistency in acting out of the highest motivation.

Flan is well known as a passionate, highly skilled and well-informed educational leader. His leadership has stretched well beyond the bounds of Scoil Ailbhe as he has given years of service to the INTO and IPPN. His authority and integrity has led to him being consulted frequently by his fellow principals on procedures and fine judgements.

Wit and good humour endear Flan to all. He has had an influence on all those who work with him giving dignity to every cause and to every colleague and student both in the workplace and in the many other circles in which he moves.

Flan has taken immense pleasure in Scoil Ailbhe's great triumphs as well as those of his own native County Clare. That Scoil Ailbhe continues to produce Tipperary players of the highest calibre is testament to his loyalty to his school, his culture and his respect for the dreams of his pupils.

He has led the transformation of Scoil Ailbhe without ever compromising the legacy of Edmond Rice. As the first ever lay principal, he has worked tirelessly with his staff to guarantee a quality education for all. Children have arrived to Scoil Ailbhe from many parts of the world and have been welcomed with open arms and treated with great sensitivity.

Flan has always been passionate about education believing firmly in children's ability to blossom if circum stances are right. He has worked consistently to bring about improvements to the buildings and investing in the latest technology and teaching methods. Although primary schools have always been short of finance, Flan has faith in people that when money is needed it will be found.

Now as his dealings with Scoil Ailbhe are done, and how brilliantly done, he leaves a legacy for all to see. We are all so proud and so lucky to enjoy the fruits of his great mission. As he writes his reflections for us we look forward to the insights he has gleaned during his 44 years as class teacher and later as principal of Scoil Ailbhe.

Miriam Butler - Principal Scoil Ailbhe

Acknowledgements

Were it not for the encouragement of a small group of people whose advice I genuinely value, this book would never have been written. So thanks to Bríd, Deirdre, Mary B, Madeleine, Órfhlaith, Dearbhla and Ciara. Thanks to Margaret for her patience and support during the exercise.

Without the I.T. skills of Aisling, Dearbhla, Helena and Mary, the task would have been far more daunting. To Noel, John and Cathal your advice was invaluable. To Brendan O' Dwyer who coordinated the whole publishing operation, your assistance was key to progress.

Responsible for the cover photography was Paddy Loughnane whose professionalism, patience and good humour added to the increasing goodwill I received from everybody from whom I sought help or advice. Thanks too to Scoil Ailbhe, Michelle and St. Patricks College, Drumcondra for the majority of the photographs. I also want to thank Mark, Shane, Jason, Patrick, Michael and Eoin (and their parents) for agreeing to make an appearance on the cover. I'll be back for you when we're making the film!

I would like to express my appreciation to Miriam for supplying the Foreword and may I wish her unlimited success at the helm of Scoil Ailbhe for many years to come. I am indebted to Michael Dundon and Declan Kelleher for their kind appraisal on the back cover. To all the enthusiastic and supportive past pupils, thanks for the considerable memories and enduring good humour. Your contributions were greatly appreciated.

Finally, to Enda, Siobhán and Dearbhla for valuable feedback. They gave the "red biro" treatment to myself for a change. Your advice, support and encouragement were significant. Ní neart go cur le chéile.

Contents

Introduction

Had I known when I started out on a career in teaching that I would be writing a book at the end of it, I believe the finished product would be somewhat different. For a start, I would have recorded incidents of note during the journey. Much of what you are about to read comes from memory.

So why am I writing a book? I am far from being a literary genius but rather I am an ordinary guy who happened to be a primary teacher. Most of the answer lies in the encouragement I have received from people, whose opinions I value, that I should put something in print. I've been told that I wouldn't consider embarking on the project unless I had a story to tell. Hopefully, that story will interest some readers be they children, parents, teachers, school staff, past pupils, future teachers, those who know me and those who don't, the people of Thurles or those who are not.

It is an account of a life spent doing a job that gave me great satisfaction. Working with a couple of generations of children was a special privilege. I trust that my interaction with them will always be seen by them as having their best interests at heart. I look forward to meeting some of them from time to time when we can both greet each other in a friendly fashion. I am pleased to say this is already happening on a regular basis.

I have, on more than one occasion, described my period as Principal of Scoil Ailbhe as being the most enjoyable of my career. The variety and challenges it threw up always kept it more than interesting. About three weeks after I took on the role of Principal, a staff member enquired how it was going and then asked me what was the difference between being an administrative Principal and being a class teacher. My response was, "You can go to the toilet in peace!" I have no doubt whatsoever there are many teachers who would forego such "luxury" for the relative – privacy – of the classroom! Each to their own I suppose.

There are numerous teachers who could write their memoirs as well as or indeed better than those recorded here. For what they are worth, these are mine. An rud is giorra don chroí is giorra don bhéal é.

Pupils of Maghera N.S. Co. Clare circa 1950. Flan Quigney in front row, third from right.

The Early Years

"Listen up now lads. Hands up if you know the answer. In which province do the Shannon, the Lagan and the Foyle all rise? Tommy?"

"Connaught, sir."

"No, Tommy I'm afraid not...Colm?"

"Munster, sir." "No...Liam?"

"Bhfuil cead agam dul amach?"

"Next please...Kevin"

"What was the question, Sir?"

I came across this scenario so often in my 32 years in the classroom that I vowed that if I ever got round to writing a book I would entitle it "What was the question, Sir?"

That time has now arrived thanks to the experience of my life and, paradoxically, one learns from one's pupils. Most people are familiar with the agony of trying to fill a page when assigned an essay in their schooldays. One of my abiding memories is of a Christian Brother in Ennis C.B.S Secondary school reading out an exceptional essay, on a fairly regular basis, from a student, with a seemingly effortless gift with English. One simile from one of those boys' essays has remained with me, where he described something as "being as useless as yesterday's newspaper". I thought, "What a genius. How do you get that sort of inspiration?" When you, dear reader, get to the end of this book I'm sure you will be able to make a judgement on whether I have made any progress some 50 years later!

Where did this idea of becoming a teacher first oc cur to me? I suppose it's a bit like saying, "When did you stop growing?" For a start there had been a pretty strong teaching tradition in my family – starting with my grand-uncle, two aunts and a cousin. In more recent years quite a few nephews and nieces embarked on the career and in my own household two of my three daughters continued the teaching career path.

I believe a person's primary school is an influence. I attended a two teacher school in East Clare in the 1950s. Electricity had still not reached that part of the world. So there was no point in plugging anything in – not even the kettle! The Principal, a native of Bantry, Co.Cork was, I be lieve, an excellent teacher. She taught Gaeilge (for which she had a special grá) with relish while she swept the floor each morning…Cuirim, cuireann tú, cuireann sé, cuireann sí… (And as she reached the step outside the door, with brush in hand and a pile of dust before it) the sound of "Arís" from her lips became fainter while we continued to recite "Arís" agus "Arís eile". By the time she reached the road, which was some fifteen or so metres away we could barely hear "Arís" but dutifully we repeated the performance! I often wondered what might happen today if the teacher directed teaching from fifteen metres outside the classroom door. I'm afraid it would be like trying to nail jelly to a wall.

Some thirty minutes or so before lunchtime the teacher, who had a few children of her own attending, would begin laying the table for the meal while she taught religion or maths or whatever. Multitasking came easy to this woman. Regularly, she would knit up a fine pair of socks or a scarf while she explained the meaning of the Possessive Case. We all thought that every teacher did this. Or perhaps we didn't think at all!

When recollecting memories from one's own schooldays it is the unusual events that stand the test of time. One such event occurred on a certain harvest morning in primary school. Those were the days when the dull sound of threshing machines caused more excitement among rural children than an ice-cream van on an urban estate. Such excitement stoked up temptation in two pupils who attended our school. Around about the same time as the Russians had launched Sputnik into the skies Pat and Breda decided they would play truant for the day. "Scheming" we used to call it or "mitching" in other parts. With the threshing machine installed in their haggard and a meitheal at the ready for the threshing, they decided they would set off to school through the fields as normal but, on this occasion, lie low in the inviting furze bushes for a spell, before returning to the threshing. The school closed for a half day, they said! Unfortunately, their oldest siblings who were in attendance at school that day, saw no sign of such concession! On arrival in school next morning the word had reached the Principal. A sturdy ruler, with at least the thickness of a floorboard, was produced. Ten apiece for Pat and Breda. The silence among the rest of us was such that you could almost hear the gurgling of the stream which meandered some 15 metres or so away. This was a record. It made an impression on us and unfortunately an imprint on two adventurous if unwise children. Unfortunately, it was a punishment (albeit severe) of its time.

Then there was Pádraig who one Friday evening, for want of something better to do, sneaked up after school hours in short pants, bare feet, icy heart and a somewhat sturdy neck and wrote an original poem about a neighbour which he posted up on the school door! Had this boy heard of Martin Luther at this stage I wonder? It read :

Tom Kennelly the big bellied man
Ate two stone of bread and a bag of bran
Two stone of potatoes and the side of a bull
And after all, said his belly wasn't half full!

Needless to say Monday morning wasn't Pádraig's favourite morning after that!

Legend had it in the locality that the same Tom had hit a hurling ball into the sky up in a place called Ruan once and it never came down! As youngsters we were never too certain if there may have been a grain of truth in it or not. What innocence!

Yet another mystery doing the rounds that time was

the rumour that three dark days would descend on the world in 1960. I well remember this prediction causing much debate among us with no little trepidation. Apparently, it was supposed to have been the third secret of Fatima! Well it was no secret now, for we had it in Maghera! Just imagine New Year's Eve in 1959 ringing in! "How long more have we?" I often used this rumour – as indeed I'm sure did many of my contemporaries – to alleviate fear in my own children when they would fearfully enquire if it was true that this disaster or that was about to happen.

There were many features of primary school in those days that seem like centuries removed from the experiences of today's children. It was not uncommon for some pupils to discard footwear from the month of April onwards and attend school each day in their bare feet. Late September would usually mean shoes or boots were restored with the onset of more severe weather conditions. By this stage the soles of the feet would have a hardened leather like texture, reasonably well disposed to defending against some thorns- mostly thistle- rough gravel and stony rural roads. Tar roads or steamrolled roads, as they were called, were a luxury for barefooted children and were not adjacent to our locality. As for myself, it was when I would have come home from school in the evenings that I would have dispensed with the footwear. I would also put them to one side at playtime, but I had a preference for protection from unfriendly surfaces while walking the mile to school each day! Towards the second half of my time in primary I bought my first bicycle and cycled in luxury. It cost £6-10 shillings. This money I had received from the sale of a pet lamb which my father gave me possession of when it was born, on condition that I would feed it daily until it was independent.

Maghera N.S. as it is today

Of course another feature of our primary school was that all subjects were taught through Irish as was pretty customary at that time. There was no doubt but that for the more intellectually able pupils this also definitely improved their grasp of Gaeilge. However, equally true was the fact that the intellectually challenged children were somewhat at a loss at knowing what was being taught.

Preparation for the sacrament of Confirmation was a serious business in those days. The sacrament was only administered to our pupils every three years. The Bishop , Dr. Rogers would examine those boys and girls who were "of the standard" while a priest would examine the candidates who struggled to retain the answers to the questions from the Catechism, stories from the Bible, miracles, parables and the relevant prayers. This examination would take place in Clooney (yes, that of "Spancilhill" fame) church on a Saturday afternoon. It was the culmination of three years of sustained indoctrination and rote learning. During the lead up to this religious test, the local priests would pay fairly frequent visits to the school to determine progress.

One such memorable visit remains with me for reasons that will become evident as you read. This particular priest, who wouldn't have been renowned for his patience, launched into examining the Confirmation class. The following exchange with a certain boy went like this:

> Priest: Well O' Brien (not his real name!) can you tell me what a miracle is?
> O' Brien: No, Father.
> Priest: What?
> O' Brien: No, Father.
> Priest: Come out here you, you.....cannister.
> [O' Brien steps out of his desk]
> Bend down there.

[O' Brien bends, the priest delivers a deft connection with his shoe to the boy's posterior.]

> Priest: Now do you know what a miracle is?
> O' Brien: I do, Father
> Priest: What is it then?
> O' Brien: Something that you'd feel, Father.
> Priest: Hmm.....sit down you cannister.

Some forty or so years later GUBU infiltrated the English language. I'm sure the incident outlined above would have qualified for that description were the expression invented at that time.

As with all primary schools of its time ours would, of course, depend for heat on a turf fire lit daily by the teacher. Parents would be canvassed – through their children- for a "creel of turf" at the start of the school year. Some parents would deliver, while others couldn't or maybe wouldn't. If a family couldn't afford a creel (a load on a cart with kind of railings to keep the turf on board) then some children would bring a sod or two in their hands to school.

Milk was the most common beverage for lunch, a few would have bottles (usually sauce bottles or lemonade bottles) of tea or cocoa. These bottles would be placed before the open fire, in cold weather, to take the chill from them an hour or so before consumption. Solid food consisted of homemade bread (usually) and butter-jam if you were lucky.

If a teacher was a married lady she was addressed as "Mam". If she was single "Miss" was the title used. "Ms. " hadn't reached our neck of the woods in the fifties! If you met a teacher ten, twenty or thirty years after you left school you still addressed them as you had done when a child. One very different aspect of today's past pupils' approach to meeting their former teachers is the ease with which they call you by your christian name. I think this is very admirable and a welcome change from the barrier-like titles of Mr., Mrs, Miss, Ms. or Sir.

Transport to secondary school was made easier for me by virtue of the fact that my late sister, Nuala, worked in Ennis and she drove me the seven miles each way every day. For my last year, when she got married, I cycled. As it

Ennis C.B.S. secondary school (Rice College)

Dr. Harty Cup semi final 1963 - Ennis C.B.S. (who defeated St. Colman's, Fermoy). Flan is in the front row, third from left

so happened it was the winter of 1962/'63 which has since gone into the history books as being one of the most severe since records began. It has regularly been mentioned when people analyse the harsh winter of 2009-'10.

While secondary school finished at four o' clock each day, for the best part of a year it would be almost six o' clock when I reached home. The journey from Ennis would be completed in about 45 minutes but while the Harty Cup campaign was in full swing we trained until about five each evening. The perk us country fellows received for our endeavours on the training ground, was a generous appetising dinner served up to us in the Monastery each day courtesy of the Christian Brothers. Now we were on an equal footing with the townies! We were fortified for the rigours of the evening and for the inevitable cycle home. Of course there were students who cycled further than me in an era of little enough traffic, but still some years before the emergence of school buses. Occasionally, I would meet old men on my way home from training on a miserable winter's evening to be met with, "Oh, this is no weather for hurling. You can't hurl in weather like this." Only for me to think, "What are they talking about? Sure it makes no difference what the weather is like." It took me years to agree that they had a point and to understand that they knew what they were talking about.

Two aspects of secondary education of that time that may come as a surprise to younger readers are that the results of public examinations i.e. The Leaving Cert and the Inter Cert (as it was then) were published in the local newspaper-The Clare Champion. All the students who attained Honours were listed first, followed by those who received passes. If a student was unfortunate enough to fail, his/her name would not appear. So, by a process of elimination, curious people could satisfy their innate curiosity!

The second aspect of the system that may surprise is that secondary schools opened for a half day on Saturdays in those times. Coming up to exam time, after Easter, we would be given voluntary (on the part of the Brothers that is!) tuition until tea-time on Saturdays. So that left Sunday only for a chance to gasp air! Now, what could one do on Sunday? Did someone mention farmwork? No chance. Sunday was a day of rest. A day for socialising. When else could you get the chance to engage in teenage pursuits?

There was nothing very revolutionary about these same pursuits. A gathering of up to a dozen youths for a couple of hours after Sunday mass, exchanging the latest banter or sharing the news of common interest. Quite often this was spent playing a game of Pitch and Toss. This game was very popular among young and old in our locality. It involved placing a prominent stone about the same size as an egg at the side of a country road. A mark would be placed about six metres from the stone (which was called a "motty"). Each participant in the game would line up behind the mark and pitch three old pennies (coppers), one at a time, at the motty. The aim was to get the penny as near as possible to the stone. The nearest penny was left to mark your progress while the two more wayward pennies were put aside for the toss. If ten people were playing, that would mean that at the end of the pitching twenty of the pennies were left aside, while ten remained on the ground to be ranked so that those who came first, second and so on could be decided. That done, the remaining ten pennies would be placed with the other twenty and the first person would be entitled to toss the thirty pennies two at a time. A hair comb was frequently used to toss the coins. If the coins fell "heads" the tosser could keep them, but if they fell "harps" they were passed on to the pool for the second person to toss them and so on, until all the coins were claimed. If anybody was lucky enough to win 240 pennies over a number of sessions then you owned a full £1! That would be enough to buy you 40 Kit-Kat bars at that time.

You might wonder were there any passing cars to interrupt proceedings? The odd one might pass intermittently but, after a brief pause, play resumed. After an hour or two either making money or losing money, it was home for dinner. It is now apparent, I'm sure, that my mother was a woman of remarkable tolerance! Adequately nourished it was back to the field for a long hurling session or if there was a worthwhile hurling fixture in Tulla it was full steam ahead to that, very often cycling three abreast on a narrow road. On the odd occasion we would encounter a Garda on his bicycle who would admonish us and advise us that we could only cycle two abreast to comply with the law. I can only imagine if people were cycling two abreast on today's roads - which are much wider-what the public reaction would be!

When we would reach our destination our bicycles would be deposited with hundreds of others in a shed adjacent to the pitch. Bicycle locks were unheard of at that time and, of course, we took the generosity of the shed's owner for granted. I'm sure we thought we were obliging her! Match over, home for tea and an energetic return to the same village, which was four miles away, to frequent the cinema. We had a reasonable interest in the film, but usually a more particular one in the emerging "talent" that surfaced when the film was over.

If we didn't encounter a Garda on the cycle home we were lucky. Some had lights on their bicycles, but many had not. How we kept between the ditches was sometimes determined by the light of the moon-if it was that kind of night-or by the shape of the hedges and trees that presented themselves as we progressed. Sometimes, to alert any pedestrian to our presence, we would whistle a modern song or a bar of the "Silver Spear" or "The Maid behind the Bar." Home safely, "the day of rest" had come to an end and it was time to knuckle down to our studies for another week.

For Leaving Cert English we had a very strict but fair Christian Brother who assigned us a considerable slice of poetry each night to be learned "off by heart". You missed it at your peril. The regurgitating of the previous night's poem kept me going – while on my bicycle – each morning until I was well beyond Spancilhill with more than half the journey done.

This was the era of the emerging Elvis Presley

and Cliff Richard, when nine Irish soldiers serving with the United Nations in the Congo were slain with poisoned arrows by Baluba tribesmen, when the Royal Showband ruled the roost, Newmarket-on-Fergus ruled the county and Tipperary's hurlers left everyone in their wake.

When I was 14 and having completed first year, my primary school Principal invited myself and a few others back to join our old school on a school tour to Dublin. Part of the tour took us to Dublin Airport. Passing through Drumcondra the teacher pointed out an impressive building to our left where, she told us, primary teachers were trained. I suppose at that stage (1959) I had harboured thoughts of gaining fulfilment in explaining the world of Nature, Gaeilge, Maths etc. to the next generation and beyond. Four years later, having completed a less than exciting, no frills and (like most schools of the time) reasonably austere secondary education, I qualified with nine other lads from the same school for St. Patrick's Teacher Training College in Drumcondra.

St. Patrick's distinctive bell tower

St. Patrick's College

The first evening we arrived in Pat's (as it was known) a new student came running down the stairs with excitement in his voice shouting, "Lads, lads there's a fella up here in one of the dormitories and he's playing a big fiddle!". So we curiously made our way up and lo and behold there was a fellow happily strumming his guitar! There were many levels of innocence in 1963. This now, was also the same summer that The Great Train Robbery took place across the water culminating in one of the biggest robberies Britain had experienced in its history!

As any teacher will tell you Teaching Practice (T.P) is one of the most dreaded and feared experiences in a young student's life! While preparing my notes for my first T.P in November 1963 news came through that President John F. Kennedy had been assassinated. It's a question that has often been posed since – "Where were you when J.F.K was slain?" I certainly had no problem knowing where I was!

For my first real T.P in St. Peter's N.S, Phibsboro, I had quite a thorough and exuberant perfectionist as my supervisor. After finishing my lesson – don't ask me what it was about – he asked me could he have a word with me (or a "focal" I think) outside the classroom door. His opening words were, "Oh, a mháistir (I was 18 now!) má leanann tú mar seo ní dóigh liom go ndeanfaimid múinteoir asat riamh!!" Meaning "Oh master if you go on like that I'm afraid we will never make a teacher out of you!!" I was distraught. A failure! Here I was, I thought, at the top of the wheel, having achieved my short life's ambition in getting into St. Pat's and now this. What a disaster! There were about a dozen of us out on T.P together. So on the way home to the college after school, on our bicycles, we started to compare notes. "How did you get on today?" I enquired of one of my colleagues. "Oh grand," was the reply, "went the finest". Same question to number two. "Ah 'twas O.K. I was happy enough now." "Oh spare us," I thought. "I'm the only f---er who messed up." I have often quoted this experience to my own children when they were growing up and facing one difficulty or another. Adults would know that there were two clear lessons here. One – and I can say it now with the benefit of experience – that my supervisor's apparent prediction was wide of the mark even if I'm sure he didn't literally mean what he said. And two, children should often take with a grain of salt the boasts of their colleagues! Chances are they are just feeling the very same way as you are.

The following summer I was doing what we call home T.P in my little rural primary school, which curiously is now occupied by a Thurles man, it being closed down as a school in 1972. True enough my famous supervisor duly arrived to see how things were going. It was a beautiful summer's day. I had four pupils. So he decided I could take them out to the doorsteps of the porch of the school. Two on the top step and two on the bottom. I taught a history lesson. He said it was brilliant. I was excellent!! Did I believe him?

Pat's gave us great memories. There was freedom. You could stay out until 10.00p.m at night and 11.15p.m on a Friday and Sunday night!! It took a fair supply of food to feed close on 250 young men. There were two Donegal boys from Gweedore at the top of our table in the refectory. When the potatoes were slow in reaching them they would scream in their best Donegal accents: "Fataí, fataí Jaysus Christ cuirigí anuas na fataí." It took me a long time to realise it was spuds that they were looking for. No TG4 in those days! The farthest away fella I heard speaking Irish up to this came from six miles at the Kilmaley side of Ennis.

Between Croke Park, Tolka Park, Dalymount Park, Lansdowne Rd, girls, dances and sightseeing it wasn't easy to knuckle down to the study . A minority of guys frequented the pub – very like today!

After the spoon fed, hothouse treatment of secondary school, it was a very different scenario in Pat's. We were now really – for the first time – left to our own devices. A good friend of mine, Johnny from Connemara, was often heard to say, "Ah we haven't done such and such, but we'll lie into it after dinner now." He was still saying that to the very end. When the meal was over on Graduation Night at the Shelbourne Hotel, with the band starting up, Johnny takes his partner by the hand, gives a wink at the rest of us and says "Come on lads we'll lie into it after dinner now". The same Johnny, being a native speaker, was often asked for his advice on certain Connemara Irish ways of saying particular English phrases. This was a common occurrence at Irish lectures with an tUasal Ó hAnnracháin. "Cad a deir sibh i gConamara, a Sheáin?" he would ask. Johnny would offer his response, which sometimes would leave the Lecturer unconvinced. With a quizzical look, an tUasal would respond with, "N'Fheadar?" to which Johnny invariably replied-under his breath of course, "N'Fheadar sa f___k!"

Friday nights were noted for dances in Conarky's (Con's as it was known) in Parnell Square, Sunday afternoon in winter for the 4 P's in Harcourt St. The Carysfort (women's teacher training college in Blackrock) girls attended here. When the gig was over, it was either a long way to Blackrock, on the one hand, with an empty stomach – or pocket – or head back to Drumcondra for the fry up from Annie! Now there was a dilemma.

My first year was the last year of the old College with its massive rambling dormitories. Rows of cramped cubicles lined the gigantic room like cars on a modern day carpark. Beside each bed was a basin and a large pitcher of water. The bell rang for Mass each morning at some crazy hour. You had a few minutes to surface before the Dean (whom we called The Bat) would whip the curtain to one side. At moments like that it was hard to decide that if you wanted a place in the sun you had to put up with the blisters. For Hedgers (as first years were condescendingly called) who rolled over for an extra five minutes shuteye, they often got a crude reminder from the Prefect who was a Gent (2nd year), if not a gentleman, by feeling the cold contents from the Pitcher on their weary faces. This Prefect was a Tipperary man. I have never met a Tipperary man – or woman for that matter – since who performed a similar method of introducing you to a new day.

A few weeks into the first term an international event took place which, among others, captivated the curiosity of all Hedgers on the dormitory floor. Cassius Clay (later to become Mohammad Ali) was fighting Sonny Liston for the Heavyweight Championship of the World. A transistor radio was unearthed. Dozens of pyjama clad figures crept through the darkness to follow the fortunes of the The Greatest. I knew nobody who favoured surly Sonny.

One of our earliest experiences in the College was that of "The Trial". It was staged in the Common Room. We were told it was an Annual Event. Judges, Barristers, Solicitors all decked out in their finest were acted out by confident "ruthless" Gents. The accused? A nervous Waterford Hedger. His crime? Charged with allegedly stealing a Gent's woman at a recent hop! The proceedings took all of half an hour at least and gleaned some mixed emotions from dubious Hedgers. Was this an act of bullying or an oversized prank? The jury was out in every sense.

There was a long tradition of Gents letting Hedgers know where their place was. Every now and then at meal time a sturdy Gents' chorus would belt out, to the air of "John Browne's Body" a powerful, forceful chant that went:

Some poor Hedgers won't be back
Here any more.
Some poor Hedgers won't be back
Here any more.
Some poor Hedgers won't be back
Here any more.
And the Gents go marching on.

This was a reminder to any first year students who seriously stepped out of line, failed their Teaching Practice or screwed up on their Junior Final exams, that they wouldn't be returning! On other occasions the chant would have a different message, this time from the Hedgers.

Some poor Gent will work for
8 pounds 10 a week.
Some poor Gent will work for
8 pounds 10 a week.
Some poor Gent will work for
8 pounds 10 a week.
While the Hedgers march along.

This was a reference to the fact that if a second year student was to fail his Senior Final that he would have to work at the unqualified rate, at the time, of 8 pounds and 10 shillings a week as against 11 pounds a week for those who passed. Only when the student repeated successfully, the following year, would he be paid the qualified rate.

Valentine's Day, believe it or not, had a mysterious veil about it – even in 1964/'65. The Bat would deliver post each morning at breakfast in the Refectory. He could aim a letter from the farthest point of the hall to land on your sausage and black pudding with the accuracy of a latter day

Eoin Kelly. On Valentine's Day he took extra pleasure in seeing the reaction of the recipient, the taunting of table-mates or the uncomfortable embarrassment of an unsuspecting teenager. Just to tease, he might circle the tables several times as an aircraft surveying the weather conditions for a descent. Then, at the last minute, he would deposit a saucy card (most certainly prearranged by giddy conspirators) slowly in front of the guy who was loudest in his jeering of others. Task completed, our Bat would wheel away with a smug smirk and a swish of his generous habit.

It wasn't all fun, of course. There was the day when, on completing his Final Teaching Practice (T.P.) for First Year, an uncertain but relieved student kicked his teaching notes up onto the nearest tree, thinking that he wouldn't be needing them again. Unfortunately for him he was called back by Independent Assessors from the Department who reassessed a cross section of students for T.P. – those very efficient , those who were average and those who were borderline fail. I'm afraid our friend was not back the following year.

Rumour had it that a few years earlier two students were sent home for pawning blankets from the College for beer money. Their career obviously took them in a different direction.

Every free hour we had between lectures was spent playing soccer on the tennis courts with tennis balls. This was and is the favoured sport of thousands of children who have and are attending Scoil Ailbhe. The accusation often was levelled that if you saw one Clareman around the College, fifteen others would follow. Security in numbers I presume, at first. As time went by though the company became more diverse. These were the days of superfluous debates over whether Man United , Liverpool or Leeds

United were the best.

The new College was completed in 1964. We took up residence in luxury, or so it seemed from the experience of the year previous. You could even place a poster of your pin-up soccer player/hurler/actress on your own bedroom wall for God's sake

St. Patricks College (Drumcondra) Graduation class 1965. Flan is in the third row from the back and fifth from the right.

Life in Laurier's

On July 1st 1965 I started my first job as a primary teacher in St. Laurence O' Toole's C.B.S, Seville Place, Dublin. It was a temporary position for twelve months but I don't think it dawned on me whether it was temporary or permanent nor did I care. It was my first job. It was in Dublin, where life was good, and that was all that mattered.

I remember being in my new class about ten minutes when the Principal came in to wind the clock on the wall. I'm sure the good Brother had the best of intentions but I thought, "He's coming in now to see how I am coping." I soon realised I was working in a very disadvantaged area of Dublin city. It shortly became apparent that many of the pupils before me came from overcrowded high rise flats, were very deprived materially and socially and were hugely affected by poverty and lack of security and stability through many factors such as unemployment, hunger and violent backgrounds. If I was prepared for this in St. Pat's, well then I mustn't have been listening that day.

Growing up in the heart of the countryside in the Mid-West, I thought every child came from a stable, happy home like my own. At about two o' clock each evening there would be a delivery of buns from Dublin Corporation to the classrooms. This was when crowd control kicked in. I had considerable experience of this at home on the farm while attempting to feed milk to 15 or 16 calves with three buckets. Try and teach the social skill of "turn taking" to a herd of calves! A useful supply of ash plants was a considerable teaching aid though. However, no such aid was permissible in Laurier's (as it was called). These poor lads were starving. And of course, it was probably the best chance of them getting a decent meal all day.

A few weeks into my teaching career I had an un-flagged visit from the local inspector who requested that I would teach a music lesson – "Ar mhiste leat ceacht ceoil a mhúineadh, a mháistir le do thoil!" So, very apprehensibly I struggled through the exercise. Right then I could have thought of numerous other subjects I could have taught more efficiently. For most novice teachers ceol was a stick-ler. Lesson over, it was fairly clear my Inspector was not too impressed. He advised me that I should attend the Music Academy in Dublin on a Saturday and learn to teach a musical instrument. Just then an alert pupil, within earshot of the conversation piped up, "Surrh, the bruda next dor has a flew (flute)". "Thank you Willie for that piece of in formation." Next business.

In the Spring of 1966 Dublin was rocked by an ex-plosion. It happened in the middle of the night. The land-mark that was synonomous with the Dublin of the time, Nelson's Pillar, had been blown apart. This was also the year of the 50th anniversary of the 1916 Rising. No doubt there was a link. I remember pupils from Laurier's bringing in small fragments of debris from the explosion to school in the days afterwards, as some kind of coveted souvenir of the occasion

Unfortunately, as was the norm in those days, it was necessary to administer corporal punishment, on oc-casion, for serious misbehaviour. When such was the case, on receiving a "slap" a child would often shout out, "Oh Daddy, Daddy, Daddy" Other teachers whom I met at the time, who were working in similar situations, spoke of the very same reaction. It took a while for us to realise that it was a repetition of a response to punishment when meted out in their own homes.

Scoil Ailbhe - Thurles C.B.S. Primary School

Settling in at Scoil Ailbhe

With no job in prospect for the coming school year and 1st July (which was the first day of the new school year in those days – now it's September 1st) fast approaching, a good friend from Connemara literally stood over me and forced me out to the phone to ring St. Pat's, in case any manager was in touch with the college looking for an "experienced" teacher. Just a few days after that phone call of destiny, I was greeted at the door of my flat by Brother Hutton, Superior of Thurles C.B.S. He was greeted by a surprised figure that had just emerged out from the bath, clad in vest and pants, hair dripping wet and side locks making good progress from the top of my ears in the general direction of my collar bone. We had a brief chat on the doorstep. He seemed to be aware that I attended Ennis C.B.S. and he signed me up for Scoil Ailbhe, Thurles as if there were only minutes to the transfer deadline.

I had only been to Thurles twice, I believe, by train

before this. Once to attend an All-Ireland Colleges semi-final in 1962 as an excited supporter, Ennis C.B.S. had recently beaten St. Flannan's by a point to win their only Harty Cup, and on the second occasion as a player in the Harty Cup Final on a wet St. Patrick's Day in 1963. I was called in as a sub with about 10 minutes to go against St. Finbarr's Farranferris. I saw the ball alright but I didn't hit it. Consequently we lost! 4-9 to 4-3. I always have great time for subs since.

A friend of mine, when I was nine or ten used to be privileged to get a lift in a car to big matches in Thurles Sports field, as it was then. He intrigued us with stories of the longest stretch of straight road (between Thurles and the Ragg, obviously) he had ever seen – possibly the longest in the world.

On a sunny evening as June was coming to an end and the English soccer team within weeks of becoming world champions, I can clearly recall walking down from Thurles Railway Station. The place was as quiet as Templederry on a Good Friday. The tranquillity was gently broken by a small group of boys hurling outside the old cattle mart, close to where Stakelum's Hardware used to be and three or four men sitting on a wall outside Bowe's. The contrast between the pace of life in Dublin was striking. Further evidence of this would be apparent in the sale of pigs and bonhams in Liberty Square on Mondays and the serenity of the children in my initial class. My first boss was Brother Corcoran. I recall being afraid to ask him when we would be getting holidays in case he might think I didn't like school!

The Thurles of the mid sixties was a world apart from that of today. Hundreds of bicycles occupied rows of bicycle racks in the school shed. Pullovers and short pants were the order of the day as exuberant schoolboys played hide and seek and determined faces fought for superiority in a springtime conker fight. Others crouched in groups to seek champion status in a game of marbles. I originally wondered how the children knew when to start the marble season. Sometime later I became aware that commercial interests dictated it.

High on the list of children's treats in those days were lucky bags, penny bars, gob stoppers and slabs of toffee. The "Our Boys" magazine was sold each month for the princely sum of 6 pence. After the arrival of the new decade of the 70's, children anticipated a Friday film in the school hall – the brainchild of the new Principal Brother Lombard. This initiative doubled up as both a useful fundraiser and as the highlight of the week for eager pupils.

Back in the classroom the usual little memorable incidents cropped up from time to time. Why some incidents remain in your head above others after roughly four decades is sometimes a mystery. Perhaps it is because some genuine "characters" were at the centre of them. One such instance occured on a very cold day in winter as I passed the cloakrooms on my way out to the playground. I thought I heard talking coming from the cloakroom. Every child was supposed to be out playing. On further inspection I spotted three boys inside. Two of them facing me saw me, but the third – a little scrawny character had his back to me and wasn't aware of my presence. Pulling up the back of his pullover and preparing himself to sit on a warm central heating pipe he uttered with much anticipated relief, "Oh Jaysus me arse is perished." "You are not serious Declan (not his name)," I said. You can imagine the reaction.

Around about this time our class went on our school tour to Dublin – the Zoo, Kilmainham Jail, the Museum were the usual haunts. Every boy went with the exception of one boy – We'll call him P.J, who was sick. The following day, as part of the follow up lesson the whole class were assigned by me to write an account of their tour. Halfway through the exercise we had an unexpected visit from the Cigire who extended his hand to me and proceeded to give it a "shake" like a wet mackerel. He took a walk around the room looking at the results of the boys' endeavours until he arrived at P.J's desk and asked, "Were you on the tour yesterday?" "No sir," replied P.J. "I was sick." "And what are you doing writing about it so?" came the reasonable retort. Needless to say I had learned my lesson. There was no delay in being informed of it too – and of course rightly so. You only make mistakes like that once.

It is only as years roll on that I now realise how different the transport scene was in the early years to what we take for granted today. Pupils from the 60's will tell you of the amount of horse drawn carts they encountered on their way to school as farmers headed for the creamery with their milk churns on board. Morris Minors, Anglias and Ford Cortinas were the order of the day. In December 1967 my late father passed away. It was only in later years when my mother, sister and brother died that I reflected on the fact that nobody from school or the Thurles area had attended my father's funeral in 1967. This, may I hasten to add, was no reflection on the relevant people but rather on people's attitude to distance at the time, the state of the roads and the quality of vehicle available. A journey that could be completed in an hour and a half nowadays wouldn't cost people a second thought now. Nearly half a century ago, there were many other considerations to be taken into account.

Around about this time I had my own first hand experience of transport difficulties. On Little Christmas Day 1969, I was returning to Thurles after the Christmas holidays when I ran into some difficulty with treacherous roads and a considerable snowfall. Going through Limerick city as I endeavoured to climb the hill which leads up towards Castletroy I encountered possibly twenty cars strewn at all angles across the hill. After much huffing and puffing I managed to reach the summit and continue on my journey. It was as I was passing Newport that I got a bright idea that I wouldn't meet as much traffic in very hazardous conditions if I turned left for the route through Silvermines! It just proves where lack of experience can get you! Shortly after, I encountered, not alone much deeper snow, but also a very formidable climb as I passed the mine itself. Try as I might to make progress the exercise became more futile. It was like trying to read a newspaper on a crowded tube train. There was nothing for it but to abandon the car and walk the two miles into Silvermines village. There I secured a bed – over a pub- for the night and, after a welcome breakfast, I walked back to my car the following morning. On the advice of my landlord (in Thurles) I turned my Anglia around and came home by Nenagh. I reported for work that morning at least an hour late but as the Principal, Brother Griffin, had got the word beforehand, he understood. This little experience has nestled clearly in my memory ever since. Most of it could happen to a young inexperienced driver today but certainly not the lodging out part as the blessing that is the mobile phone would surely have come up with some solutions for a rescue.

Transporting a cat in the boot of a Ford Anglia from Clare to Thurles would probably land one in trouble with the I.S.P.C A. Such an attempt – with unpredictable consequences – took place in the winter of 1968. An arrangement had been made that I would take a cat from my home place to a friend in Thurles one weekend when I was returning. The animal was loaded up and I set out on my journey accompanied by my nephew, Fintan, who I was to drop off at his home in Limerick city. We had a brief stop in Quin where Fintan had to leave a message for a cousin. On arrival at my digs – O'Meara's on the Racecourse Rd – I opened the boot to fetch my cat. Nothing. Searched inside the car. No luck. I came to the conclusion that Fintan, must have inadvertently let him out while taking the message to the cousin. This was now Sunday evening. On the following Saturday I had reason to open the boot of my car when I was nearly rocked back on my heels by a demented, psychotic, scrawny figure of a cat with a body like the blade of a farmer's scythe. With one gigantic leap and a screech that could have carried to Boherlahan, he disappeared at lightening speed into the distance in the direction of the Hospital of the Assumption. Apparently, he had made his way out of the boot, in behind the back seat of the car, and there was me going up and down to school every day for a week, driving here and there as you do, and completely oblivious to the ferocious fears of a feline!

One of the best descriptions of a child's progress was given to me around this time. We still had no formal organised Parent-Teacher meetings in the 70s. A mother knocked at my classroom door one day to ask me how Joe was doing. I said that he was doing really well "Up there in the top four or five," I told her. " Well you know," she said, "We were thinking that alright, but you know tis like a calf you'd have at home in the yard, you'd never know how he'd measure up until you bring him in and 'shtand' him in the mart."

In the seventies, Thurles Drama Group performed many plays in Scoil Ailbhe. In 1975, they performed Bryan McMahon's play "The Honey Spike". I was playing the part of one of the Travelling People in it, and succeeded in securing suitable clothing/costume material from a woman living a few miles outside the town. She was to leave them for collection, by me, at Gleeson's shop outside the school. She understood this to be Gleeson's in Rossa St. outside the C.B.S. Secondary School. So the next day I visited Gleeson's shop outside Scoil

Ailbhe – the C.B.S. Primary School - and enquired if anybody had left any clothes for the play for me. I was told no but just then I spotted a suitcase left on the floor of the premises. I took a look inside and sure enough there was a great supply of gear within. Old shirts, socks, trousers, boot polish, long johns, the lot. "God" I thought, "This poor woman went to great trouble for me".

That night was opening night for "The Honey Spike." We got off to a brilliant start. Relief all round. Next morning Brother Lombard called me down to his office to inform me that, "There is a man here who said that you had taken his clothes the night before". He further added that, as a consequence, he (the man) had to spend the night in the Hospital of the Assumption and that he now wanted them back as he was on his way home to Kerry!

At this time Boards of Management first came into being. At a meeting of I.N.T.O. delegates from Tipperary, Clare and Waterford held in Lahinch in June 1975, which I attended, the composition of the new Boards were up for debate. The granting of a primary degree – the B.Ed – was also welcomed at that meeting which pointed out that this had been sought by the I.N.T.O since 1908. Other topics discussed at that meeting were (i) Pupil Teacher Ratio (what's new!) (ii) Teacher Supply – no teacher coming out of training in 1976 (Because of the increase in years of training from two to three) (iii) The future of the Seventh Class. One delegate raised the problem of "assessors" (who were local clerics) at interviews in a West Clare parish handing candidates the tonic sol-fa and asking them to sing hymns!

The contribution that female teachers could make to Scoil Ailbhe was acknowledged with the appointment of the first lady teacher Mrs. Gertie Ryan in 1968. Writing in "Memories of Scoil Ailbhe" (A book published in 1999 to commemorate the 50th anniversary of the school) former Deputy Principal Muiris O' Cléirigh wrote, tongue in cheek, "Many changes have taken place over the years, but none as shocking as the appointment of women to the teaching staff." Then there was the lady Cigire who nearly sent poor Bro. Corcoran to an early grave. He doubted that she was in the right school and said that we never had a lady Cigire before, to which she replied that "He had one now!"

In the early 70's some whole school tours to Knock Shrine in Co. Mayo were organised. On one such occasion the details were revealed to staff and pupils alike. We were to leave by train from Thurles station. Teachers would also have to pay their way, we were told. I questioned this. I considered it was enough to marshal, supervise and look after a sizeable group of children on a long journey for a lengthy day without having to pay for the privilege as well! I was told there was no way out of it. So the stubborn streak in me decided I would check with the Railway Station to see if this was indeed the case, to be informed not at all, there was no necessity for staff members to require a ticket while accompanying the whole group of children.

Equipped with this information I notified the relevant person that I would not be travelling to Knock but that, of course, I would be attending school to look after those boys who were not travelling. Which I duly did.

Letter re: The Sale of Work

The following is a copy of a letter I recently came across. It gives a flavour of the time.

THURLES C.B.S. PRIMARY SCHOOL FUND

Guidelines for Parents and others who wish to donate goods for C.B.S. Primary School Sale of Work to be held on SUNDAY 27th APRIL, 1975.

STALLS AS FOLLOWS:
FLOWER AND VEGETABLE STALL –
Cabbage, turnips, potatoes etc.
BOTTLE STALL –
Lemonade, Whiskey, Wines, Bath Lotions etc.
DRAPERY STALL –
All goods in drapery line appreciated for this Stall.
MINERAL BAR – Minerals, Ice-Cream, Crisps, Buns etc.
TOYS – Of all description.
20p STALL – Bundles of comics, books, beans, soap, talc etc.
CAKE STALL – For parents and others, who have not got time to bake, please send in sugar, margarine, self raising flour, fruit etc. Please send these one week in advance to give ladies who have offered to bake an opportunity to do so.
WHEEL OF FORTUNE – Towels, table linen, tea sets, bed linen, sets of drinking glasses, boxes of groceries etc.
Goods for sale of work will be gratefully received at Christian Brothers' Monastery (residence)

Health and Safety - Then and Now

I suppose one of the many great changes that have taken place in education over the decades is the enormous heightening of the awareness of the necessity for more stringent measures to improve the health and safety of our pupils. A vivid memory of my own days as a primary pupil was of a regular request from the teacher for a few other boys and myself to scour the surrounding fields, hedges and ditches to secure some firewood for starting the school fire for the following week. This always happened on a Friday evening around two o' clock and while school was over at three, we sometimes didn't return with our loot until 3.15 or 3.30 just dumping the sticks, or "faggot" as it was called, outside the school door.

For many years in Scoil Ailbhe – certainly for my first twenty years there – it was fairly common for a boy to require stitches as a result of a hurling accident. A teacher, usually the Principal, would take the boy across the road to the District Hospital, as it was then, to receive medical attention which frequently required stitching. With the great benefit of hindsight one would have to conclude that, apart from the discomfort of the poor victim, this was a huge waste of time and resources for both the hospital staff and the accompanying Principal. The introduction of compulsory helmets was a Godsend and since that regulation I have never seen a boy require stitches as a result of a hurling accident in the school.

The practice of using pupils as altar servers was very much in vogue up to about 1988. These boys left the school each day to serve at daily mass, funerals or weddings. Not all at the same time, I may add, but many boys would be required at least once a week. They would be absent form school for an hour on average and I have little doubt that they were not too upset if there was the odd delay, and who could blame them. Saturday masses and those celebrated during school holidays were conspicuous by the absence of altar boys!

I believe there are a few areas in the Ireland of today where this tradition remains. I look back now and just shake my head. There is an old saying which says, "Custom reconciles us to anything". And it is so true. You could apply it to slavery, the confining of Croke Park to the staging of G.A.A matches only, or the use of altar servers during school time. Apart altogether from what the children missed in terms of education, there was, of course, a considerable health and safety risk here as well. What would happen if a boy was knocked down going to or from the church or was exposed to any other hazards? Principal Bro. John Hickey pulled the plug on this practice shortly after he took over and the world didn't stop spinning the following day!

In the distant past, occasionally a "responsible" boy was sent on an errand outside of school. A teacher friend of mine tells a story of how the father of a well known footballer, called to the school one day to ask if the Principal would allow Paul to take a trip out to the adjacent field now and again during the day to keep and eye on one of his cows which was due to calf at any time. Time went by anyway and there was no sign of Paul returning, so the Principal and Paul's brother took off to locate him, only to find Paul staring over the newborn calf endeavouring to ease the transition for the little creature before Paul himself would return to class! Needless to say I couldn't see this happening today.

Only in the last seven or eight years have the children from Scoil Ailbhe been prevented from leaving the school environs at lunchtime. As the school caters for boys from 2nd to 6th class the tradition going way back was to allow them home for lunch. However, as times have changed, lunchtime is halved, the volume of traffic has snowballed, there are fewer dinners in the middle of the day, children are mostly driven to school nowadays and so the need to release pupils to their own devices midday has dwindled. Throw in many more risks attached to young children getting the run of the town to themselves in 2010 and a decision to confine boys to the school ground becomes a no-brainer. From the early days of college we were always reminded that the school is in loco parentis. After all, our duty is to protect. As the saying goes, "There is only one pretty child in the world and every mother has it".

Which brings me to an interesting school tour of the 80s which occurred on a few occasions back then. It was an exciting tour of its time, but would scarcely pass the litmus test for safety in modern times. One of our teachers of that era familiarised me with the details recently. This teacher and his class of about 35 pupils took off on a school tour on their bicycles to climb the Devils Bit Mountain. To anybody not too familiar with the geography of the area this would be a trip of about 24 miles – 12 there and 12 back. You could just imagine 35 boys on bicycles, cycling together on a narrow country road being marshalled by a responsible teacher, who was doing his utmost to slow down the boys at the front and to spur on the guys at the rear. If it was nowadays we could expect to see a Garda outrider at the head of the troop with a couple of more Gardaí bringing up the rear. The Principal was to follow on in his bus – Tour de France style – in case there were any casualties.

They arrived at their destination in style, had a picnic, climbed the mountain and with strict instructions not to put a foot on a pedal until they had descended to level ground, all was going to plan. Or was it? One particular adventurous sort didn't hear the instructions, or didn't heed them. So he took off, increasing momentum as he sped, crashed into a bend on the boreen and was tossed into a bed of nettles. Luckily the Principal arrived in his mini-bus in the nick of time and looked after the distraught little mountain climber.

Nowadays, we have 24 hour Personal Accident Insurance Schemes available in schools to facilitate parents who wish to join them and quite sensibly many do. Within the last year two other teachers and I defended an allegation, in court, being made by a mother on behalf of her son, who claimed that he had suffered an injury in the class room on a wet day when children weren't allowed outside. She claimed that this injury occurred because there was not sufficient supervision in the place at the time. It came as a considerable reassurance to us in the school that the judge concluded that we had, indeed, adequate supervision in place and duly dismissed the case.

It's not unusual ...to be given a laugh!

Over a lifetime teaching there are many serious situations on a daily basis. Little surprise in that you might say. Education is a serious business. Every now and again a little funny incident helps to keep the spirits up and fortifies you throughout an occasional day which otherwise might be as grey as a January twilight. I often regretted not writing them down as they happened and I would strongly advise any young teacher to do so and indeed for teachers well into their careers it is never too late to start. Some that I have retained from memory are as follows:

1972 was a significant year for Margaret and I, because that was the year we got married. However, it was for another reason that I mention it here. A popular song at the time was "It's not unusual to be loved by anyone". There was one boy in my class back then who entertained us all with his impression of Tom Jones. The dreaded leather was a feature of some schools in those days, ours being one. So the impressionist would use the leather as a microphone and wriggle and gyrate as Tom Jones would do to the sheer amusement of his captive audience who would be literally rolling around their desks with laughter.

For nearly as long as I can remember, while I was a class teacher, the latter part of my Friday evenings was given over to debating. The format was very much in the style of the modern television programme "Questions and Answers". At the top of the classroom we had a panel consisting of about five pupils while individual topics came from the floor. Topics varied over the years, naturally, but some of those which often emerged were: "Should the Gardaí be armed?", "The Northern Ireland Troubles", "It is an advantage to be famous" , "Should some rule or other in G.A.A/ Soccer/ Rugby be changed" etc, etc. On this particular day the topic was "What does the panel think of bullies?" When the boy asked the question I interrupted to clarify it saying. "Now you could put that another way…." "Yeah", piped up the class wit "What do bullies think of the panel!" In ordinary life it is common place for some people who don't want to, or can't answer a question to buy time, very often by asking another question while they think. One such occasion was when I was examining tables one day. As usual the questions were flying thick and fast. "Six nines? Four nines? Eight nines?" as I moved from pupil to pupil until I arrived at this little traveller boy with "seven nines?" He looked at me for a split second and then said, "What d'you mane seven nines?"

Much later when I became Principal of the school I was cycling up to the front gate of Scoil Ailbhe bright and early one morning. Waiting for me to open the gate was one smart little boy who might have reason to be familiar with pub talk from time to time! On seeing me arriving on my bicycle he shouts, "Were you put off the road sir?"

Then there was the boy who towards the end of the year in the middle of a lesson rose to his feet with a camera while I was in full flow and clicked.

A precocious little fourth class man had an unusual habit. Each morning as I would be going from desk to desk correcting work, he would catch my tie as I leaned over his copy and twirl it making a "prrr" sound.

Beside the school is a sportsfield called Páirc Ailbhe. Thurles juvenile camogie teams down the years get to play matches on it. Came a time when preparation was being made for an important match and a mentor came to me and said, "Have ye nits down in the school Flan?" Surprised I replied, "Ah...not that I know of."

"Are you sure?" she asked. "God, not that I'm aware of now." I suggested."I thought the last time we played a game down there we had the nits," she insisted. "Oh! NETS?" I said (with some relief). "Oh we have indeed," I said, "I'd forgotten there for a while."

Finally, there was the day when the teacher next door was telling his pupils about the Dead Sea. He said there was so much salt in it that if you went swimming in it you could actually lay back and float on your back looking up at the sky. There was this boy in the front seat who was unconvinced. "You could I'm sure," he said sarcastically, "the whales would ate the arse off you!"

The launch of "Memories of School Ailbhe 1949-1999" at the Anner Hotel, Thurles, with Rev. Br. Anthony McDonnell (Provincial of C. Brothers) and Most Rev. Dr. D. Clifford, Archbishop of Cashel & Emly

All in the name of progress

The scale of change in terms of resources, facilities, customs, curriculum, methodologies, administration, Departmental legislation and communication (in its broadest sense) in my teaching career has been revolutionary.

In terms of teaching aids, every few years saw a new invention which made life that little bit easier. For example, the facility to duplicate documents was a major breakthrough. A gestetner, cumbersome and all as it was, first made an appearance in our school in the 70s. For a number of years in the 80s if you wanted something typed or photocopied you availed of the services of the Teacher Centre – as it was then called – in the town. This was located on the top storey of a four storey building overlooking the Suir. While it was a welcome service, you wouldn't want to be in a serious hurry with your work and the climbing of substantial stairs must have been an endurance test for many. However, 1991 brought huge relief with the purchase of our very own photocopier. Could we manage for five minutes without it today? – ten at a push!

Up until the 1980s the school phone could only receive incoming calls. Unbelievable this may seem today. Did children get sick in those days? How were parents contacted? Then again not many parents had phones in those far off days. Of course, this crazy situation was a reflection of the lack of state funding at the time. Contrast this with the availability of phones today not to mention how many mobiles the average household has at their disposal.

The 1980s was also the decade when A4 paper made its appearance, largely replacing its predecessor the foolscap. How long could any school – or indeed any organisation – last without the A4 sheet today? In 1983 we introduced Homework notebooks.

During my first ten years teaching, the adding up of the attendance figures in the school roll book at year's end was a considerable challenge. There were so many numbers to be added that you would need the brain of a mathematician. The busy hum from forty five pupils within hours of summer liberty was not the most facilitating or soothing backdrop either! But hurrah! Here come the mid 70s and calculators. What clever devices! No need to employ teams of pupils to come to my assistance anymore. Will anybody add 2 and 3 in their head from now on?

The first third of my career saw us teaching pounds, shillings and pence as well as Imperial Measurement such as tons, cwts, miles, furlongs, yards, etc.1971, heralded the introduction of decimal currency, with change again occurring in 2002 with the onset of the euro.

Fast forward to the middle of the 90s and along comes a computer. "What can we do with that?" we thought. The I.C.T.

revolution was about to begin, e-mails, laptops, scanners, computer room, hardware, software, megabytes and whatever you're having yourself. And finally in 2009 the very essence of Information and Learning – the Interactive Whiteboard.

Anybody between 25 and 40 would surely have remembered the projector (An teilgeoir) and deilbhíní for the daily Ceacht Gaeilge. I know. You didn't like them. Perhaps "didn't like" wouldn't be your favoured description?

Uniforms were introduced to Scoil Ailbhe in 1990. The advantages were obvious. Everybody was equal. There are no designer uniforms. Well at least I don't think so.

Monthly confession for all classes in the Cathedral of the Assumption was commonplace up to about twenty years ago. Since then the local priests visit the school for the sacrament.

For a number of years in the 70s a formidable Alsatian guarded the school. Even the resident mice lost the will to live in those years. At that time and for many years after, no keys were available to staff members. Too bad if you forgot to bring home your bundle of copies for correction. When you were out, you were out. The Principal and the cleaning lady were the sole keyholders. Once I took my life in my hands and having secured a key from the genial cleaner I ventured back in to carry out a particular task. Unfortunately I was found out and let's just say I behaved myself after that.

The Centenary All-Ireland Hurling Final between Cork and Offaly took place in nearby Semple Stadium in 1984. For many years Principals Bro. Keane and Bro. Hickey organised, together with the Thurles Sarsfields club, the selling of programmes for all the big matches staged locally. The senior boys from our school were the main programme sellers during that era.

Pupils who encountered serious difficulty with literacy and numeracy were handed a valuable lifeline in the 70s with the establishing of the Learning Support service in some schools. However, children with Special Education needs had to wait two more decades before Resource Teachers were appointed.

The practice of streaming children i.e. determining classes by intellectual ability came to a halt in our school about a quarter of a century ago. The 70s saw staff taking tea breaks for the first time just as pens with nibs and manufactured ink gave way to the smoother biro. Another practice which came to an end at that time was the visits of the Archbishop of Cashel and Emly, Dr. Morris, to the classrooms to examine the Confirmation children.

Curriculum changes brought an end to the Primary Certificate in 1966. A new Curriculum arrived in 1971. This heralded the recognition of such "new" subjects as Art & Crafts and Environmental Studies. Subsequently, a revised curriculum was introduced in 1999.

A secretarial service, under the F.Á.S. scheme was set up in 1995 while our school had been granted our first Department funded Caretaker some thirteen years before hand.

A significant development took place in 1982 with the ending of Corporal Punishment. I know the last boy whose misfortune it was to receive such a punishment from myself. I doubt if he realises that he was the last! One way or another it was an enlightening and reforming move which has certainly benefitted society. There may be some who will disagree. A case again of custom reconciling us to anything. Even though I only administered it for serious misbehaviour, I would have preferred it was banned before I commenced my teaching career. At the time, we thought one couldn't survive as a teacher without resorting to corporal punishment for maintaining order. Time has shown otherwise.

Like many others of my age and many much younger, I was on the receiving end of the stick and leather during my school days. Incidentally, perhaps that was one very significant reason why third level was so different and refreshing. However, there is one slap – a "sog" , we used to call it – which stands apart in my memory. It was about ten days before I sat my Leaving Cert. We were revising our Maths – on a Saturday with a brilliant Maths Teacher and Christian Brother. He was, and still is, a man for whom I had great time. He was giving us voluntary tuition, outside of normal school hours and was passionate about his subject. He asked me a question, by way of revision, which I didn't know. He called me up, gave me an unmerciful belt of the leather and stuck it back in his pocket again. I was 18 years of age, my hand throbbed but I still didn't know the answer to the question. The only thought I had in my mind was: How futile? That thought remains with me even though I know full well why the man reacted in that way i.e. frustration at my ignorance despite all his hard work.

The Education Act, 1998, put Education on a statuary footing for the first time. This was followed by a raft of legislation such as the Education Welfare Act, The Equal Status Act and so on requiring the need for greater responsibility, accountability and administration and the paper work involved is a serious source of frustration for teaching Principals in particular who have to immerse themselves in it after they have finished teaching their pupils.

Staff at Edmund Rice's house in Callan, Co. Kilkenny 1996.

A Day in our Class – 6th Class 1988-'89

Just over 20 years ago our school's Parents' Council asked me to write an account of what an average day in our school was like. The following was what I wrote. I applied it to events in my own class because that was the scene with which I was most familiar:

Ours is an urban school of approximately 450 boys. I normally teach sixth class. The following fictitious names represent some of the characters in the average mixed ability sixth class: - (a) Colm, brilliant, keeps your heart up, is sometimes bored I imagine, there are two or three like him. Doesn't have to over exert himself. (b) Liam listens all the time is very attentive. There are a few in this category (c) Noel – talks to his neighbour at every given opportunity. He rarely, does much. There may be six or seven Noels. (d) Matthew is dead sound, average intelligence, will never mess and is very co-operative. His type is the backbone of the class and is definitely your friend. (e) Jim is a smart ass. He thinks he is born to entertain. I have never met a class without one Jim and many have two. He is an awful burden on others and is an obstacle to progress. (f) Tom fiddles all day and scribbles whenever he gets away with it. He is often bored. He cannot keep pace. There are six or seven Toms. (g) Kevin represents the five or six who are just be low the top group but who give everything 100% effort.

The 8.55 a.m. bell puts a scatter to our staff room. Class begins at 9.00 a.m. We begin with morning prayers. Labhairt na Gaeilge is next. As the children are now at their most alert stage , this is the most suitable time for an

Ghaeilge O Bhéal. The boys in two of the three rows say a few sentences about anything they want to as Gaeilge. The boys in the third row question them on their contributions. Roles will be reversed in the following days. It's 9.15 a.m. Tom arrives. He slept on it, he says. Noel is wondering if his neighbour is going to the Spring show. 9.20 a.m. is time for correction of homework. First we check the Maths. Then we check any other written work given.

The boys get a chance to look over their spelling while I see each boy's homework. Tom has only two of the five sums done because "somebody" said that "we had, only two to do". Noel left his bag in his mother's car and when he wanted to do his homework she was gone to Bridge. Mothers always make a mess of things! I can guarantee you they are a much maligned group in every class. They didn't leave out the swimming money and they didn't give him the envelope for his report etc. Noel is already at the line for continuous talking. Seal ag Leamh next. Things are going nicely. Jim produces the inevitable compass as a learning aid! I take possession. On opening the window, aim for the griselenia below and hit the target with the swiftness of a Ryan-Air jet. It has now joined the red plas tic soldier, the kinder-egg cover and numerous conkers. Please forgive me Gerry Daly. (A gardening programme presenter on T.V. at that time).

9.45 a.m. – Now for the spelling test. We have two teams, competition is razor keen. However a check round the class is vital in case Noel has already written out the list before we start and is ready to do a discreet mime. The lads are generally quite honest. They correct each other's test. However, this needs to be supervised regularly just in case there is a bit of "you scratch my back and I'll scratch yours". I call the roll while the test is in progress 32 in, 2 out. The "number" boy arrives with the mission box and number book. Tom slips a 20p coin through the slot. This is a regular occurrence and speaks for itself.

Buntus next, Noel yawns. Tom slips the refill from his Bic and tests it on his Religion book. Jim is wondering if "Gearoid" in the filmstrip is a lick because he is picking up the teacher's glasses in the ceacht, " Obair Bhaile". The bell rings. Its time for Sos.

If it's not my turn for yard duty I have a break and a chat. 11.00 a.m. – the bell again. Round two Maths. I used to teach Maths after dinner for years, I've changed timing. The reason being that the noise level is lower and concentration is higher before lunch. Tom punches holes in the twelve milk cartons, inserts the straws and at least twelve lads are happy. We're doing Profit and Loss. I explain the sum. "Any questions?" I ask. Two boys ask questions. "Any more?" No. Away we go. One minute later, "Anybody in trouble?" Ten hands go up. I call them up around the blackboard and we make great progress. It's a lovely informal little group. We could make tea at a moment like this if there were only eleven of us. Meanwhile down at the end of the room Jim passes a note to Kevin wanting to know, "Would you go with Jennifer?" I spot him. I'm aware that the Department of Education has a guideline on discipline which says that under no circumstances is ridicule or sarcasm to be applied, so I just say, "Jim you are not to do that now, good boy!!"

The bell goes at 11.50 a.m. This is normally time for Religion. Five of mine leave for Remedial English so as its Confirmation year we do Geography now and leave Religion until after dinner. There is a good interest in Geography. Maps take many a boy's fancy. We also do History some days at this time. This varies. Colm wants to know about Socialism, while Tom is drawing a picture of Iron Maiden. Liam explains the Home Rule Bill while Jim says his mother is baffled by the E.S.B. bill. As this is Jim's thirteenth time interrupting he is now moving close to a red card and extra homework. 12.20 p.m. – dinnertime.

1.20 p .m. – signals the end of lunch break. 450 kids line-up in the yard. The three teachers on yard duty send the pupils to their respective classes. The next couple of hours are very demanding. It is much harder to drive home the message. Young minds are now tiring and beginning to wander.

I recently asked a fourteen year old girl what she would like to do when she grew up. She said, "I would love primary teaching". I said, "Do you know that it is much harder to teach in the evening than in the morning?" She said that she didn't. Of course this was no surprise. Neither did I when I was fourteen.

Religion first. It goes well. Most get involved through discussion or asking questions. Today we are do-ing "Toleration of People who differ from us." Matthew tells about the Protestants he met in Enniskillen when his Daddy was up buying the television set. There are nine boys at the line who have missed their questions once again. They have just joined Colm who has dug a ruler into Kevin's ribcage.

English now and five of the lads leave for Remedial Maths. Jim, Noel and Kevin want to know, "Bhfuil cead agam dul amach?" We round off the lesson with written work. They need a break from my voice. Noel wants to know "are we going swimming tomorrow?" Tom wants to know, "When are we going on the school tour?" Diversion makes a bold bid to take over now unless kept in check.

2.45 p.m. We are doing P.E. today. Liam, Tom,

Kevin, Colm and Jim volunteer to get the mats. There is a distinct air of letting off steam now. Tom springs on the trampoline like a gazelle on an Ethiopian Plateau. Noel is smiling like a cat in a creamery. 3.10 p.m. – the bell for the end of the contest. We return to the classroom, say our evening prayers and line-up for the walk to the cloakrooms. There is an air of relief among young and old. I return to the classroom to close windows etc. Lo and behold the clock is ticking! Thank God for the gift of sleep. Why? Because those 32 kids who were so wound up leaving school this evening will be new boys, relaxed and refreshed at 9.00 a.m. tomorrow after ten hours good sleep hopefully.

Some observations about working with children

As my own children at home went through the education system it became clear to me that one of the most useful skills a child can learn at primary level – or indeed at any level – is the skill to have the ability to summarise an article, a story, or an account of something. That is to be able to pick out the important points, to edit or to give a synopsis of a piece of writing. In my time in secondary school we used to call it Précis, I believe.

There are several opportunities in life to put this skill into practice. It is regularly called upon by students researching a topic at third level, be it in the library or through the internet. Even if you are giving directions to somebody on the side of the road it is useful to be able to cut to the chase.

This became very apparent to me when I was teaching sixth class. Every day one boy would be given that day's newspaper to pick out any item that interested them and write an account of it in a short summary. Certain children could rise to this challenge easily while many would much prefer to read you out the whole news item word for word – if they got away with it!

Young teachers do not take long to discover that most children have little difficulty answering a question that has the answer available in the structure of the question i.e.

THE SINGER TRAVELLED BY RAIL TO THURLES ON SATURDAY?

Who travelled?	The singer
How did s/he travel?	By rail
To where did s/he travel?	To Thurles
When did s/he travel?	On Saturday

However when the question Why? is asked, it creates a difficulty and calls for more thought and imagination. Of course, any parent with a very young child will be well aware that when faced with the question, "Why?" some serious level of language and imagination is called for!

This question, "Why?" reminds me of a question I was frequently asked over the years, "Sir why was Jesus born in Israel"? To which I invariably replied, "Well if he was born in Norway people would ask why he was born in Norway. He had to be born somewhere." I was never too convinced that my answer adequately fulfilled the curiosity of the questioner! Another famous one was, "Sir what's your favourite band?" The expected reponse was supposed to be U2, Westlife, Status Quo or whatever the trend was at the particular time. My response was, "The Moycarkey Pipers!" I was regularly reminded that they never made the charts!

I was always amused by a certain answer I received in a Religion class. It could be termed an "old reliable". When I would ask how many boys in our school could show love for Jesus or show the world they were Christians the "old reliable" would be offered year in year out, "Sir you could help an old lady across the road". To which I would say, "I see, and did you ever help an old lady across the road?" Boy: "No Sir".

F.Q.: "And did you ever see any boy from this school helping an old lady across the road?"

"No Sir".

"And neither did I, since I came to Thurles. It's a lovely thing to do but I'm not sure it happens often. Think of any other way lads".

And so on. I often wondered about the origin of this noble aspiration but whatever it was, it surfaced every year without fail in my class.

There are many factors which affect the progress of children educationally. Most of those are dealt with elsewhere in this book. However, it is essential to mention here how important a child's attendance record is to his/her progress. Quite recently, there was much debate about 4,000 students failing maths in their 2010 Leaving Cert Examination. That figure represents about two students in a class of 30. It would be interesting to determine what part attendance at school all the way up from primary school played in that result. A poor attendance record, of course usually goes hand in hand with a serious lack of motivation. For that matter the lack of a Learning Support service dedicated specifically to maths at primary level is surely a factor.

From my experience working with boys-and I have not taught girls-I have observed that a high percentage of them (maybe 90%) will just do enough to get them through school and keep themselves out of trouble. Having listened to parents, teachers who teach in mixed gender schools, and having three daughters myself, it is pretty clear to me that girls, in general, are certainly more motivated. Sorry lads now, but there is substantial anecdotal evidence available to support this theory! A case of the world being full of willing people, some willing to work and the rest willing to let them!

In the mid 80s our school embarked upon a pilot programme in the sixth classes which was different. Up until that time, streaming children according to ability was commonplace. However, around about then many educationalists put forward the view that teaching children through mixed ability groups was educationally more advantageous.

By way of compromise, the local inspector of the time suggested that the three teachers in 6th class would pilot a method which involved some of both theories. He suggested that each of the three teachers, including myself, would have a core class of our own each day up until lunch time. During that early part of the day we would teach subjects such as Geography, History, Religion, P.E. Environmental Studies etc.

To facilitate the afternoon programme, the children were graded according to ability in the core subjects of Irish, English and Maths. For my own part I had the group which was above average for Maths, the middle group for Irish and those who required extra teaching for English, the second teacher took the top group for Irish, the middle group for English, with Maths at foundation level and so on with the remaining teacher.

How did we find the experiment? Well it was the first time I had to move to different locations on a daily basis. This was also the case as far as the pupils were concerned. There were 117 children in the three classes that year. For the afternoon sessions there would be, on average, 2/3 of the group who didn't belong to my own core group. So they would have seen me only as a Maths/English/Irish teacher. Very much similar to the post primary system, I'm sure. I would have to say that personally, I found the teaching of Maths to be a rather "isolating" experience, if that is the correct description. By this I mean that the children could contribute little by way of stories about the material being taught. Call it interaction, if you will, compared to that experienced when teaching English, Geography, Nature etc. My apologies to all Maths teachers who vehemently disagree!

Punctuality in starting and finishing classes was a must for all three teachers. If you had to wait a few minutes outside somebody's door, that was a new experience, indeed, for a primary teacher! The personal tastes of indi vidual teachers, which never concerned us up to this point, now took on a more significant meaning. One teacher fa voured plenty fresh air while another may prefer a higher degree of heat. Each teacher also had his own particular form of blackboard management unique to himself.

From time to time I would encounter a parent who would enquire how their son was doing at Maths (for example). If the boy was not in my core class, it would take me much longer to be familiar with his progress than with the old system. Come to think of it. It would take me longer to know his name!

When the inspector returned at the end of the year, needless to say he was very interested in our evaluation of the system. We informed him of all the negatives which I outlined above, which he took on board. He then asked me for some positive feedback. I told him there were results which I considered to be positive. Those were that, for the first time ever in a given year, I knew everyone of the boys in sixth class. Furthermore, if there was a troublemaker evident, he saw less of me during the day and I encountered less of him!

What did all these pupils think themselves, I wonder and how beneficial was the system to them? I do not have a definite answer. However, I suspect that if the three teachers were unfulfilled, there is a strong likelihood that that would have filtered through to the children. Suffice to say that the following year we reverted to mixed ability teaching which continues to the present day.

Talking to children at their own level is one of the earliest requirements for anybody dealing with children. This is why so many teachers engage in the use of analagies while communicating. Occasionally, somebody who isn't used to dealing with children might visit a classroom to announce some event or competition or other and leave delighted with themselves, only for the children to raise their hands as, the visitor has exited and ask, "What'd he say Miss?" "Where's it on?" "What time are we to be there?" etc.

So what are the things that are important to children? Well have you a week? Well for a start it is widely recognised that children learn best when they are happy. They respond very well to praise and a nice little smatter of humour. It is quite some years ago since I had a visit from a mother who said to me, "Ye seem to be always laughing!" It kind of crossed my mind for an instant, "God this woman must think we are just dossing in here." Nonetheless, I gave her the benefit of the doubt and was satisfied that there was no such inference on her part.

On the third last day before I retired, 240 boys presented me with two albums containing letters, poems and little tributes. It was a memorable gift, very much treasured and appreciated but tucked away here and there in the albums were indications for me of little things that children rate and value highly. These little things are true of any child in any school, in any county in Ireland or in any country in the world. I repeat some of them below:

- An expectation of sorting out a bullying issue
- Recognition of good behaviour – awards, certificates etc.
- Support at matches
- Grub after finals!
- Fairness, calmness, kindness, a sense of fun.
- Not being shouted at.

This is also an opportune time, to list a few requirements that children need in school in order to make progress as mature, well rounded citizens: consistency, security, firm but fair discipline, good example, very clear guide lines on what will and what won't be tolerated and regular reminders of how to respect all those around them, young and old alike.

In another chapter I will deal with the ways that children vary – very often, or indeed, mostly due to life's circumstances.

All of life's a stage

As a youngster St. Stephen's Day meant two things to me – going out with the "Wren" during the day and setting off to see a play on St. Stephen's Night. The play was an annual event in nearby Tulla and those stage performances instilled in me a life long love of drama. Shortly after coming to Thurles I joined the local Drama Group and the Musical Society. I have some terrific memories of both but as my first love was for drama, I was involved in something like 16 productions in all with the group between 1969 and 1984.

Formal and informal drama would have featured considerably in my teaching career also. When first we attended St, Pat's all those years ago, we were regularly advised that many aspects of the school curriculum could be very effectively reinforced through the informal use of drama. I'll be honest and confess that at that stage I was unconvinced. As time went by of course, it all made sense as from the earliest years, children thrive in the world of make believe and if they can learn better in the process all the better. Millions of children watched Sesame St. in their youth, yet were oblivious to the fact that they were actually learning valuable facts unknown to themselves!

The Annual Christmas Concert in Scoil Ailbhe I'm told kicked off in the 50's. An older teacher once told me that even the odd power cut didn't interfere too much with the entertainment, as a couple of cars in the school yard were started up and the resultant light from their headlights enabled the show to resume and continue until the restoration of power.

For the pupils themselves the concert was one of, if

Playing the part of Michael Cusack - with a group commemorating 'GAA 125' in a reconstruction of the inaugural meeting in Hayes Hotel on 1-11-1884.

not the highlight of, the year. Once rehearsals began, giddiness and hyperactivity were as predictable as snow on a mountain top. For weeks before, the School Hall was timetabled for rehearsal and each class had its own timeslot. An air of unsurpassed excitement invaded the place. I knew of many teachers who suffered this annual letting off of steam with the enthusiasm of a canary in a coalmine, while many others thrived on it.

When the curtain went up each year (although in later times it was every second year) the hall heaved with anticipation. Parents, grandparents, family, past pupils and friends thrilled in the performances of all but, of course, especially that of their own special little superstar. Many returned the next night consumed with pride, overcome with laughter and liberated from their own individual worries for these couple of hours. As ours was an all boys' school, particular enjoyment was always obvious among the audi ence when some of the lads dressed up for female parts. Of course the following day every teacher was told that, "My parents said ours was the best, teacher."

However, one thing is certain the confidence gained by these children or any child – performing, is invaluable. New scripts year in year out were always a challenge but some teachers had a flair for writing their own scripts and so what could seem a problem on Monday, might well be nothing of the sort by Sunday. What might not always be known, is that not every child wants to do a speaking part – many do, but a certain amount are much happier to decline one. However, most children are game for anything. I once remember doing a play about a school tour to Dublin. There was a scene in it where the pupils were visiting the Wax Museum. I had one boy playing a statue of Nicky English, (famous Tipperary hurler) but it didn't dawn on me that the particular lad was out sick until the class and I were on the way down the stairs to the hall to perform. So I met a boy from another class (whom I taught the year before) coming up against us and I stopped him and said, "Hi Damien will you play Nicky English for me". "No problem" he said, so away we went and he took to the part like one of these mo-tionless performers you associate with Shop St. in Galway.

How often have we heard that every teacher would need eyes at the back of their head? Well I experienced something akin to that as I was saying my final few words on stage at the end of one particular Christmas Concert. As I thanked the usual people I noticed the audience started to giggle and laugh. So I said to myself, "I don't think I'm that funny." I carried on with my speech for a moment and again another burst of laughter. This reminds me of teach-ing a lesson, when all of a sudden the class erupt in laughter and you straight away have the intuition to know that some guy topping a pencil behind your back thinks he's Mr. Bean. So glancing back over my shoulder I saw the head of a long "giraffe" (is their any other kind?) disappear behind the curtain. I knew then that the Staff's own Mr. Bean was up to one of his regular pranks!

Talk to any past pupil and they will all reminisce with fond nostalgia the twists and turns, the ins and outs of the Christmas Concerts they starred in while attending Scoil Ailbhe. Whether they assemble at Weddings, or Christenings, pubs or clubs, filling stations or Garda stations, stag nights or rag nights, birthday parties or sleepover parties the verdict is still the same – they were just mighty!

For more than twenty years now our school has featured a Poetry Morning. Again this is a morning of high humour, imaginative acting and stimulating poetry. It's a morning when what seems but lines on a page, can be taken by the scruff of the neck and made stand up and walk, cry, scream, beg, entertain or do scores of other activities. It is an hour of enchanting entertainment that can remove an old fashioned perception of a poem into something far morc relevant and, in many cases, much more interesting, hilarious and humorous.

"Play on", says the referee

My love affair with the game of hurling dates back to thrilling encounters in the primary school (national school we always called it then) playground. Hurleys were few and far between in Maghera N.S., the "crook" being the instrument wielded in pursuit of the ball. Most "crooks" were fairly similar in design to the Scottish shinty stick but certainly not nearly as refined! I know the temptation here is to ask was there ever a youngster who shared a similar title with this particular version of a camán? Perhaps the teacher of the day had a view on that but it will remain unrecorded.

The first club match I witnessed was in Dr. Daly Memorial Park in Tulla where St. Joseph's took on Whitegate. A neighbour's van was the mode of transport – two men in the front and a friendly fox terrier and myself in the luggage compartment at the back. Later my cousin, John, would carry me on the crossbar of his bicycle the whole seven miles to Cusack Park in Ennis and back again, just stopping at a steep hill outside the town – a welcome respite to ease the pins and needles on numbed limbs. In later years I wondered how many adults would go to such rounds and hardship for a child of six or seven.

Just like many youngsters of today, hurling was practiced religiously from dawn to dusk. It has often been repeated and has the air of a cliché about it but I suppose we hadn't very many choices to pursue a wide range of other pastimes. Further whetting the appetite of an impressionable youth for more excitement was a journey to the Gaelic Grounds in Limerick in the company of the same John and my father to see Clare sneak a surprise victory over Tipperary (1-6 to 0-8) in the Munster Semi-final of 1955.

Munster Final Day July 1995. The day the revolution began

Some might think that it was fate then that landed me in Thurles – the very home of hurling. My own theory would be that Thurles was sufficiently removed from the hardships, drudgery and monotony of spending one's leisure time on a 60's farm.

Is there another town in Ireland to equal such a hurling tradition as Thurles? I doubt it. There are more All-Ireland medals in this region than there are vertical telegraph poles. Thurles C.B.S. itself is steeped in the game and has produced a plethora of serious exponents of the camán. Thurles C.B.S. primary – Scoil Ailbhe is synonymous with hurling. Successive enthusiastic Christian Brothers nurtured the ancient game through the early years and that love and passion has been carried on by very dedicated and committed lay teachers.

Initially, school leagues with teams called Tipperary, Cork, Kilkenny, Limerick, Clare, Wexford etc. were the ultimate in competition and pupils battled and fought for supremacy like ferrets in a sack. A retiring teacher, Willie

O' Dwyer (R.I.P.) who had an unrivalled grá for the game dedicated the Corn Ó Duibhir cup to the school as a further incentive for pupils to pursue their favourite game. My own 6th class boys often competed ferociously in The Tayto League! This was long before Allianz, Heineken or Etihad came on board! The 70's saw more regularised competition with the establishment of Cumann na mBunscol. The school competes in both football and hurling competitions under its auspices. On close examination of the inscriptions on the "A" Hurling Trophies the name of Scoil Ailbhe will feature more often than that of any other school.

Past pupils of the 80's and the 90's in particular have fond memories of "rallies" in the school yard before Finals with chanting, singing and rousing encouragement with the competing team standing on the elevated platform at the top of the playground. Their favourite memory of those exciting days was of the whole school chanting, "Bang, bang….. bang, bang, bang,……bang, bang, bang, bang…Scoil Ailbhe". In more recent years an indoor version has often been repeated in the school hall.

Over the last fifteen years or so, one of the most anticipated events of the school year has been the Yard League. This is a hurling league played over the winter months in both school yards immediately after school on two evenings a week. Every child from 3rd class to 6th class is eligible to play, and it is contested with the ferocity of the Champions' League. On final day, a great friend of the school, who is a member of the famed Moycarkey Pipe band, leads both teams on to the playing arena. Pupils, parents, grandparents, past pupils, teachers, secretaries, caretakers, special needs assistants and curious bypassers all vie for a prime vantage point and while cheers wrestle with tears at the finish, the world seems to stand still for 30 minutes at that hugely significant occasion in the tender lives of Tipperary's future sticksmen. And not always Tipperary's, occasionally, an elusive medal escapes over the border to Kilkenny or even further afield to Poland, Latvia or Lithuania. Spreading the gospel to the latter states is one thing but now Kilkenny – that could be another story!

There are many boys in the school who bring their hurley and helmet to school as often as they bring their schoolbag. Their hurley is their badge and I have no doubt many of them lay it to rest at night in their bedroom.

Great credit for the development of Gaelic games within the school goes to the aforementioned highly enthusiastic motivated teachers who give hours on end of their spare time to the promotion of the sport. Likewise credit must go to an exceptionally good coach, Paddy, who works with the boys weekly courtesy of Dúrlas Óg and Bord na nÓg.

Being a Clareman living in Thurles has always been a source of banter within both the school and the town. One incident in particular sticks in my mind. In the Munster Semi-final of 1987 Clare and Tipperary drew in Killarney. The replay was won with considerable ease by the Premier. I remember going into class the following morning with the scoreline printed in large script on the blackboard:

Tipperary 4 – 17   Clare 0 - 8

The boys rubbed their hands with glee at that one!

At the height of a particularly keen rivalry between Tipperary and Clare over ten years ago, a staff member was heard to say to me, "I never knew that there was a special rivalry between Tipperary and Clare, did you?" I answered that I did, and on being asked why that was so, I went on to explain that this happens in any sport where you have one very successful team and another one quite starved of success. You can call it an inferiority complex, if you like, on the part of the underdog and a certain confidence and expectation from the more successful county. However, this situation has greatly changed since Clare's All-Ireland triumphs.

I can say from personal experience that I never experienced anything but respect and fairness by Tipperary supporters over the years, laced with a fair dollop of the usual slagging and ribbing that is part of the G.A.A. Occasionally, you will get one yob here and there but I'm certain you will have the equivalent on the other side of the Shannon. What hasn't helped matters is the nonsensical contributions (from time to time) by a few commentators in the media and elsewhere, who like to keep the pot boiling. There are always a few on both sides who rise to this rubbish. I'll leave the final word on this matter to my good friend Declan, former I.N.T.O. Executive Representative for Waterford, Tipperary and Clare and a former I.N.T.O. President – a Clareman himself. Declan covered thousands of miles through these counties and beyond during the course of his work and I've heard him, on more than one occasion say, "If my car had a breakdown in the middle of the night there is no greater place to be assured of assistance than in Tipperary". What is obvious is the knowledge, love and appreciation people have in Tipperary for the G.A.A. and in particular for the game of hurling.

Once or twice people not too familiar with the game will say, "What are you doing supporting another county? Aren't you living in Tipperary for a lifetime?" To which I reply, "Aren't you from Moycarkey, Loughmore, Holycross, Boherlahan or wherever, do you support Thurles Sarsfields?" To which I get a very definite reply. Such is the tribalism that contributes to the intrigue of the G.A.A. You

County Final Day in Semple Stadium

don't wake up some morning and say "You know what? I think I'll support X from now on". If people can support soccer teams from Liverpool, London, Manchester, Sunderland or Birmingham – and in some cases never set a foot on such places – is it any wonder then that people born and raised in a certain place have a special affinity for it? As I've already said, that's what makes the G.A.A. unique.

However, as would be expected, not only the G.A.A. held the interest of many boys in our school. As in schools throughout the world, soccer ranked highly in terms of popularity. At no time was this more apparent than in the lead up to the 1990 World Cup Final in Italy- Italia '90. Jack Charlton was in the height of his reign and our near neighbours and age old rivals, England were in the same group as the Republic.

The trouble was that home games were played in the old Lansdowne Road which, at that time was not equipped with floodlights. Consequently, games had to be played early in the afternoon around 2p.m. In 1989, Ireland were hosting England in a crunch qualifier in Dublin. The lads in my class had their eyes out on sticks to see the game on television. I can't speak for boys in other classes, but I can imagine they were the same. It is only fair to say that this "child" writing this account here and now was as bad as any of them! So I planned to take them to the video room to see the action. However, this decision did not impress in certain quarters, who used their "muscle" to convey the message to the appropriate authorities to inform me that showing such a game to my class during school hours was against Department regulations and was not allowed! I was stunned. I was deeply hurt. Needless to say, the boys were bitterly disappointed also. For the record, the final score was: Republic of Ireland 1 (Cascarino): England 1. I suppose what disappointed me most was, that considering all the times I would have worked above and beyond the regulated time, this decision was not taking cognisance of my contribution. If I was a dosser, well fair enough. I can fully understand, of course, how the boys in other classes would have felt if mine were allowed view the game, but there was a solution to that. Show the blooming thing to all and sundry. I'm sure the Taoiseach of the day was at the game - and maybe the Minister for Education for that matter! – and I would have little fear that they made up for the time lost later.

So that was it. I made a particular protest, which I am certain made a very significant point. How do I know this? Well the next home qualifier game in which Ireland were involved was beamed into the School Hall, on a big screen, with the whole school in attendance and I'm tempted to conclude by saying – and they all lived happily ever after............. well nearly all.

May they rest in peace

At approximately 9.10 a.m. on Friday December 12th 1997 the phone rang through to my office. It was Thurles Garda Station. The voice at the other end conveyed the message to me that there had just been a serious accident across the road from the station. The Garda said that it was believed to have involved a member of my staff and that he was knocked from his bicycle. He also asked me if I could inform his next of kin.

Anyway you look at it, this was devastating. The whole school went into shock. The unfortunate victim, of course, was none other than our esteemed Deputy Principal, Fintan Brennan. Fintan, an Ennis native, took up his first job in our school in 1957 and had served loyally and with some considerable distinction until that fateful day in December 1997.

As I moved through the school to inform the staff, I noticed that Fintan's class were still lined up in the yard awaiting collection. They were looking forward to their Christmas Concert and especially to their own item "Oisín i dTír na nÓg." As Fintan cycled to school that morning he, too, had his mind on this production and was planning to put the finishing touches to the famous stone which is synonymous with the legend.

For as long as I knew Fintan, the trusted bicycle was his mode of transport. It was tragic beyond belief that a car door opening onto his path was to prove fateful. Two days later Fintan passed on to the great classroom of eternity.

So many boys had been put through Fintan's hands coupled with the fact that he was widely known, that the whole town of Thurles and indeed much of Tipperary, his native Clare and beyond were stunned beyond belief. He was a man, who had an uncanny interest in people, but in particular children. Past pupils regularly speak to me of his kindness to them and of his gentle encouraging ways and, of course, of his deep love of hurling, golf, singing and music. Writing in Memories of Scoil Ailbhe in 1999 I wrote of Fintan, "The Late Bryan McMahon, teacher and dramatist, wrote in his book "The Master" that a good teacher leaves the track of his teeth in a parish for three generations. He could have been talking about Fintan."

Monday 20th March 1978 was no ordinary morning in my sixth class classroom. Far from it, there was a chilling atmosphere and numbness about the place. You see the previous evening there had been an accident and one of our class, Paul, had tragically lost his life. Like many of his friends, Paul had been returning from a Cross Country race meeting in Kerry when approximately nine or ten miles from Thurles their bus left the road and came to a stop in a nearby field. Paul was the sole fatality.

The sombre news had a profound effect on the town, his school and indeed especially on his classmates not to talk of course of his devastated family. These boys all formed a guard of honour at Paul's funeral and marched with his remains to his burial place. On that morning I remember asking the boys to pray for Paul's soul, when I was interrupted by a very mature and thoughtful boy, Aidan, to remind me not to forget his parents and family also. It was a memorable moment that has remained with me. I may have been getting round to that stage of the prayer but I was very impressed by the presence of mind and responsible attitude of a boy so young. Later on that year our youngest daughter was born. We christened her Ciara Paula.

The late Fintan (fifth from left) on our way to the 1989 All-Ireland Hurling Final

Thankfully, that was the one and only time, in a lifetime teaching, that a pupil died while still in my class. I am grateful for that but naturally would be happier – as would everybody else – if the statistic was zero.

Unfortunately as with other schools, there have been other tragic situations where children lost their lives. Funerals of past pupils whose lives have been snuffed out suddenly, are of course hugely traumatising and deeply sad occurrences. Then, like many other work places, our school was gripped from time to time with profound sorrow for staff members who had lost loved ones near and dear to them. The deep faith and resilience of those bereaved is not just a continued source of wonder but also a subject of our greatest admiration.

The Principalship

When the Trustees of the Christian Brothers decided in 1997 that the next Principal of Scoil Ailbhe would be a lay person, it didn't take very long for me to decide I would be applying for the position. The Christian Brothers had contributed enormously to education in Thurles since the first school was founded in the town in 1816. Not alone that, but I had been involved with them either as a pupil or as a teacher since the age of 13. A new era now beckoned and it was up to me to prove if I could lead the transition and meet the challenge.

Including my year in Laurence O'Toole's, I had served under nine Principals – very good Principals, good Principals and Principals. Surely I must have picked up some leadership skills along the way and discarded those which did not appeal to me? I was reminded of a quote by one of the American Presidents which said, "There are three kinds of leader – those who make things happen, those who let things happen and those who wonder what's happening!"

When interviewed for the position of Principal, one question I was asked has remained etched in my memory. It was, "If you were appointed Principal would you expect to know everything that goes on in your school?" I think it was a super question and I often thought of it over the following thirteen years. The answer I gave was what you would expect, "Yes, everything of relevance, surely"

A few days after I was appointed I asked my sixth class boys for suggestions concerning how they thought a Principal should perform. As usual I got a variety of opinions on what sort of person a Principal should be. I decided that Eoin's was the pick of the lot. I got it typed up and it was displayed in my office until my retirement. It read, "The Principal should be fair and not very strict, but at the same time, not let people away with murder. If there is a serious problem he should deal with it and not let it prolong. He should get involved with the school and get to know what the students are like. The pupils can often be fond of someone who makes a good joke every now and then. Also someone who doesn't lose his cool over nothing, but takes serious matter seriously".

On starting the job two wise sayings often came to mind which ring true of any leadership position, "When people stop bringing you their problems you cease to be their leader" and "The leader of the orchestra doesn't have to play every instrument".

In the years up to this I can safely say that I had differences of opinion with only two or three parents. Within the first six months of becoming Principal that number would have increased fivefold. There were two reasons for this development. One, just like a new full back in a rugby team he will be tested with a few early high balls to see what he is made of, and two, while you may have a problem child or two in you own class, as a class teacher, now, all of a sudden, the corresponding children in every other teacher's class were ultimately your responsibility. In other words you had inherited a kind of a NAMA like situation! But not to worry, if you weren't aware of that scenario beforehand, well you shouldn't have put yourself forward for the position!

I remember somebody saying to me around about this time, "Well I wouldn't have your job for any money". The same thought had occurred to myself one day while I was walking through Glasgow when, on looking up, I saw a huge crane over a building site with a man half way to the moon astride on it and I thought, "Well I wouldn't …..etc. etc." I'm sure if you were to wait long enough for him to return to earth and asked him would he like to become a school Principal he would surely come to the same conclusion as I came to about his chosen career.

When I was a class teacher myself, I gave very little thought as to how I received a Principal when he entered my classroom. Was he made feel welcome? What did my own body language say? Only when one becomes a Principal does awareness of such mannerisms become reality. While I'm on this subject the teachers, in our school at any rate, showed enormous levels of patience considering the huge volume of interruptions they encountered on a daily basis. What they probably wouldn't know is that their teaching style would have some influence on the Principal's interaction with their class during some of his visits.

There were occasions, while teaching, when I would look out the classroom window and see the Principal drive out the school gate and think, "That's not a bad life!", while I was slogging away at the Briathra Neamhri alta. However on becoming Principal myself, the day I had to leave the school during the course of the day, was the day I was least happy. When I say this I know only too well, of course, that responsibilities outside the school are an essential part of the role. Attendance at Child Protection Conferences, matches, seminars, inservice courses, court cases, funerals, Principals' Conferences, visiting local schools on school business etc. was absolutely vital and a necessary function of any school leader. That said, I always felt that in the school, at the coalface, was where I was needed most and furthermore, for every hour you were away, there was every chance that your workload later that day would also have increased by the same amount of time as that which was spent elsewhere.

It scarcely needs emphasising that having a pivotal role in the appointment of staff is one which demands a high level of responsibility. Teaching and learning is a serious business. Children deserve the very best. Both they and their parents are entitled to it. Hence, I may be stating the obvious when I say that candidates must be appointed on merit. Strange as it may seem – and maybe it is not so strange – but there is a certain belief among some that the old nod and wink culture is alive and well. "Have you any influence with the Chairperson, the Principal or whoever!" Or "you owe me a favour" etc. "X is interested in that job now and I went to school with his/her mother." To sum up, the same principle should apply when appointing staff as applies in the classroom, i.e. treat everybody the same.

The Principalship can often be associated with isolation and even loneliness. This perception comes about, I'm sure, because quite often one has to deal with confidential issues. Occasionally, you cannot discuss the information to hand with anybody else. Quite often, it may be something you may only share with your Chairperson until such time as a Board Meeting is called.

However the support of other Principals I have always found to be invaluable of course, a supportive friend is as vital as a control tower is to an airline pilot. It gives extra credence to the adage that no one can be happy without a friend, nor be sure of them till they are unhappy.

"Cowboys and Indians"

The inevitability of its unpredictability is often a phrase used to describe the Principal's job. One can never be certain what will happen next. This theory was truly borne out one morning when I had a visit from an Indian gentleman who wanted to share his skills at Art and Craft with the staff. He first demonstrated for me in my office what he had in mind. He could make some beautiful floral designs, with coloured paper, and suggested if he could demonstrate the skill for the staff, then they, in turn, could use it to good advantage in their next Art and Craft class.

After some consideration, I agreed to let him talk to the staff as break time was coming up. Break over, teachers impressed and our friend agreed to give one further demonstration in one particular classroom. What I didn't know was that his main intention was to sell the Instruction Manuals he had with him to the children for £2 each!! The conversation in the room went something like this:

Ranji: Excuse me Mr. Hynes (not the teacher's real name) I am being very happy to be selling these boys my little book for just £2.

Mr. Hynes: Gor I'm afraid Ranji these lads don't have any money with them

Ranji : That is little problem. You see unfortunately I am not being able to come back tomorrow as I am flying out to Munich this evening.

Mr. Hynes : Oh that's a pity. Sorry about that now.

Ranji : It is no problem. How many boys are you having in your class?

Mr. Hynes : 32

Ranji : So you will be giving me £64 and I will be
giving you 32 booklets and these lovely boys will
be giving you back the money to-morrow O.K.?
Mr. Hynes : (Slightly apprehensive…no, very ap
prehensive) O….K…. but…(handing over £64)
…but
Ranji : Now I go to next class. Bye must rush
now (Exits class)

Mr. Hynes, putting two and two together, steps out of his
classroom and on descending the stairs meets myself on
the way up.

Mr. Hynes : Flan, that Indian chap has collected
£64 from me already for those craft books and
he's now gone into Peter's class (not his real name
!) to sell more
Flan : He is in his f—k !! (Knocks on Peter's
door)   Excuse me, sir. Now take yourself out of
this building now while you're able. Come on.
Out ! (or words to that effect)

This incident is recalled with some glee by the staff
members of our school who were there at the time. It has
been dramatised on two occasions to date. Once when Mr.
Hynes was celebrating a special occasion and secondly at
my own retirement party!

Parents in Partnership

That the support of parents is an essential element in the progress of a school going child is as well known as that Jack and Jill went up the hill. Supportive parents ensure that a child is confident and reassured and leads to successful educational outcomes. Support, of course, will largely depend on trust and as we all know trust is a two way street. If the school can deliver an admirable satisfactory education then support from parents will usually be a given.

However, there are always situations where, for a variety of reasons, a minority of parents, while wanting to support, may find themselves unable to do so. Herein lies the challenge for any school and teacher.

Communication is such a vital component in any school or for that matter in any organisation, business, Government, home or family. It is crucial for the effectiveness of the whole operation. There are dozens of angles to communication be it, "This way to the office" signs or how you receive the salesperson but what I have in mind here is keeping people in the loop. Generally speaking, if people are kept in the picture, numerous misunderstandings are avoided, even conflict is averted and people will reciprocate by keeping you, in turn, in the picture. Of course we all know there are exceptions, but this is as true of parents as it is of staff. If a teacher doesn't get the full picture on what is going on in a child's life outside of school then misunderstandings may arise. Conversely, if parents feel certain information concerning school hasn't reached them the same is true.

The Parents' Council in Scoil Ailbhe have been doing amazing work for nearly a quarter of a century now. They have been to the fore in areas such as Book Rental Schemes, the sale of Tracksuits, Graduation Nights for 6th Class boys, Dog Nights, Fashion Shows and Who Wants to be a Thousandaire?

Were it not for the support of parents in the area of transport it would have been difficult for our teams to compete in games throughout the county.

Most parents understand that rules tailored to suit hundreds of children may vary slightly from rules governing two or three children at home. I have to say that the friendliness of grandparents at the school always impressed me – or was it that they were looking at a grandparent themselves?

A very significant development in the welfare of children took place in the late 80s and early 90s with the adoption of the Stay Safe Programme (S.S.P.) onto the Primary school curriculum. This could not have been brought about without the support of sensible parents. The Stay Safe programme gave children the vocabulary and strategies necessary in order to equip them to protect themselves against child abuse. In the light of all the reports on Child Protection/Abuse that have come into the public domain today, it was one of the major developments in children's education.

Unfortunately, it did not come easily. A stubborn campaign was fought around the country against the S.S.P. by some right wing "religious" groups who sought to "protect the innocence of children" It gives me the greatest pleasure to say that myself, and others, vehemently disagreed with their views and together with many others promoted it stringently in our schools. I often wonder what those fanatical protesters of the early 90s think now.

During my time as Principal it was always a pleasure to meet up again with past pupils – many of them reappearing as parents. Those of them who were operating services were also of great assistance to the school in their capacity as electricians, architects, plumbers, carpenters, lawyers, accountants, photographers, journalists, business people, priests, painters, plasterers and so on.

While there were no female past pupils, the nearest I came to the equivalent were those camogie players I eoached for some seven or eight years. Some of those fly ers of 1987 – '95 have now returned as parents, one or two reminding me of the U16, U14 and U12 County Camogie titles won by Thurles for the very first time.

No school can function effectively without a supportive and co-operative Board of Management. There have been some outstanding Board members in my twenty years on the Board, all selflessly giving of their time vol untarily. The school is indeed indebted to them. The success of any Board is to have membership free of vested interests. Once that has been established, the management of the school will normally flourish.

From time to time parents will inevitably have grievances. It is essential that parents make a prior appointment with the Principal. In the vast majority of cases, in my experience, a reasonable solution was found. Whereas the occasional and very rare "morning ambush" is doomed to failure as logic usually goes out the window at that stage.

Parental concerns in relation to bullying are very real and understandable and as this is an area in which I have a special interest, I will deal with it in another chapter.

For the most part, I have found parents to be supportive, kind, friendly, co-operative and obliging. They expected a good education for their children and were entitled to receive it. On the very odd occasion when I was at the receiving end of a serious verbal attack, it became clear shortly afterwards that it was some issue totally outside of school related matters that was the real issue which caused the outburst. It is well for any person dealing with the public to be conscious of that fact – difficult and all as it is to understand that at the time.

There have been sporadic complaints made to our school over the years. Any teacher will tell you that one positive statement makes up for the many negatives. If I was to list all the flattering things that were said over the last few years I'd be accused of boasting, so I will give a few of the other kind – just to keep our feet on the ground :

"What kind of a f------ school are you running here?" (after his son was suspended for serious misbehaviour)

"I'll report you to the Board of Education" (after her wayward son was reprimanded for the umpteenth time)

"Ye's are all a shower o* pr----" (after we failed to find a time suitable for both parties to resolve a problem with a disruptive child)

*This word delivered with a strong Northern accent and rhyming with "quacks"!

87

Some thoughts on Bullying

One of the most common concerns parents have when their child enters primary school is the fear of that child becoming a victim of bullying. By bullying we mean sustained deliberate, aggressive acts which are intended to cause distress, harm or damage to victims. These acts may be verbal, physical or psychological and can be brought about by innuendo, lies, harassment, intimidation or indeed physical attack. I am not talking about a once off, isolated incident here. Not that that can be in anyway condoned either.

Unfortunately, there is not a workplace, school or college in Ireland that has not experienced bullying behaviour at some stage of its existence, be it perpetrated by adults, adolescents or by children. Most people realise the consequences of this despicable behaviour. Some of these would be the dismantling of confidence and self-esteem, feeling of worthlessness, guilt, helplessness, shame, losing one's appetite, feeling sick, loss of sleep, panic attacks, nightmares, problems with behaviour, bed wetting, depression or, as we have seen in the more extreme cases which have made news headlines, even thoughts and acts of suicide.

The tactics used may involve cruel strategies specially planned to frighten, upset, exclude, undermine, isolate, insult, physically injure or emotionally scar the unfortunate victim.

No child should have to put up with being tormented in such a fashion. Schools can play a leading role in greatly diminishing the climate where bullying can thrive and I know schools are much more aware of this insidious problem nowadays than, I believe, was the case many years ago. This is indeed in line with society in general.

In 2002 I attended, together with another teacher from our school a Conference on Educational Disadvantage in St. Patrick's College in Drumcondra. There, we came across an interesting concept which was being practiced in a school in Dublin, by a Parents' Group. It was the idea of an Anti-Bullying Week. This was a week that would be set aside annually to heighten awareness among children of the problem of bullying. That bullying thrives on secrecy is as well known as that a child grows up to be an adult. So that very fact in itself was important to be highlighted for children.

Since that Conference in '02 an Anti-Bullying week has been part of the Scoil Ailbhe culture ever since. Teachers hold detailed lessons on what constitutes bullying, reasons why it can happen, its effects, when and where it may happen, the different roles which can be played by children which can allow bullying to prolong, who are likely to be victims, what drives the perpetrator, how the victim feels, the different methods of bullying, strategies to prevent same and so on. Side by side with these lessons are art lessons, essays, slogans etc. to heighten awareness among the children.

In more recent times one of our teachers with a special interest in the area did some extra research on the subject and introduced an expanded programme for teachers to deliver a comprehensive message.

My own experience tells me that while name calling in itself may not always lead to bullying it is the single most annoying and demeaning habit among some children and is at the root of most trouble. I have often said to children that not only is it a prime cause of trouble in schools but that it is very frequently the catalyst for trouble/violence in clubs, pubs, fast food restaurants, playing fields, parties and on the streets of probably every town and city, not just in Ireland, but worldwide. If name calling can be the source of conflict and hurt when children (or people) are sober think of what the effects are when they are not.

We often think of just the bully and the victim being the only players involved in this cancer. In a group or class situation there are many others who usually play a part. Quite often there is a core group, who fear the bully and therefore give more indirect but tacid support to the perpetrator. Then there is a cohort of pupils who are aware the sordid business is going on but decide it's none of their business and carry on with their own concerns. Next we have a group (or maybe one) who will decide to talk to a colleague about it but who may be afraid to take direct action and finally, hopefully, that last action link in the chain will take the bold, but crucially essential step and inform a responsible adult be it a parent, a teacher, a staff member or the Principal.

They key skill in all of this is to tell on the bully. I have rarely met a child who is prepared to tell easily. Most fear the repercussions. This is a serious mistake. If handled properly by those in authority there should be none.

Not long ago I talked to all the classes in our school who had been made aware of the various groups that can play a part either directly or indirectly in bullying. I asked them how many of them had witnessed a situation such as that since they enrolled in primary school. In every classroom, the result was the same – approximately one in three were familiar with it.

It is also very important to say here that when the episode of bullying is reported and dealt with, in 95% or more cases that is the end of the matter. I would always ask parents to ring back or call again if there is a recurrence. Otherwise one could assume the matter was resolved. Quite often, and indeed in most cases, the perpetrator doesn't realise he is causing the victim such suffering and is often quite remorseful.

It must be all of 25 years now since a mother visited me at my home one night to report that her boy who was a pupil in my class was being bullied. Obviously, she was afraid to come to the school for fear of being seen by her son. There should be no need for anybody to take such precautions nowadays. An appointment with the class teacher or the Principal is the recommended route.

In conclusion, I would like to pay tribute to a small group of parents known as the Supportive Parents Group – who have over the years done invaluable work in meeting the parents of 1st class children, who come to Scoil Ailbhe from the other two feeder schools in the town. – Scoil Angela and Scoil Mhuire. Their role is to ease the transition for these children and to help to allay the concerns of new parents who may not be too familiar with the school. Part of that role also is that of reassuring parents that an effective Bullying Policy is in place.

Some of the lighter moments

Pupils versus teachers hurling clashes were a feature of Scoil Ailbhe in a period somewhere between 1998 and 2004. They were always a source of comedy and high jinks laced with beads of perspiration and buckets of en deavour (by some)! A report from one such clash circa 1998 went something like this:

The teachers' dressing room was downbeat and still in the aftermath of a dogged struggle. A spectator seeking access to what was now the losers' sanctuary knocked apprehensively. "I'm in the shower", came the reply from within. "After a performance like that you're lucky you're not in jail", she retorted as she disappeared into the masses.

The venue was the inside yard of Scoil Ailbhe last Thursday where the teachers threw down the gauntlet to the cream of the school's young hurlers in a pulsating challenge in aid of the Romanian Children's Appeal Fund.

The groundsmen had been erecting crowd control barriers since early morning such was the expectation and interest of the young and some of those who just thought they were young. A beautiful trophy carved out of three different kinds of wood awaited the winners and a dubious "mushroom" for the losers. The partisan atmosphere made Ibrox or Parkhead seem like an evening by the river.

The pupils were first to emerge onto the arena to tu multuous applause. Brendan (capt.) was followed by Richie, Brendan, Muiris and the brothers Colin and Andrew.

To a cacophony of boos and catcalls and clad in the Blue and Gold of the Premier County the teachers lined out as follows: Mr. Ryan, Mr. Sheppard, Mr. Kerrigan, Mr. Quirke, Mr. Hanrahan and Mr. O' Reilly with Mr. Bourke

(Manager) making a very questionable substitution late in the game by introducing Mr. Quigney.

After the contest it was generally accepted that D.J. made the right decision – Get out while you are at the top! Final result:

Pupils: 10 goals Teachers: 9, and a welcome cheque for the Romanian Appeal Fund.

Another event which was highly successful (from a charity point of view) and popular among the children – and among staff who would be willing enough to admit it! – was a pupils non-uniform day combined with a staff fancy dress day. Here, staff dressed up in costumes which portrayed characters such as Goldilocks, Little Red Riding Hood, Superman etc. As our postman wisely commented, "The lunatics have taken over the asylum here!"

End of term/ year staff outings became common place during the 80s. In the earlier years both the primary school and the secondary school staffs were guests of the Christian Brothers community down in the monastery at Christmas time when we would all be treated to a four course dinner topped up with refreshments. Afterwards upstairs an M.C would be appointed and a long night of music and song would ensue. This was a very generous gesture by the Brothers and no doubt set them back a quid or two in financially difficult times.

In later times "nights out" consisted of the usual meal capped off with a sing song.

In the last fifteen years or so with the age profile of the staff lowering, more "active" excursions took place such as boating, pitch and putt, go cart racing or golfing. The sing song element faded and was replaced by stand-up "comedy", charades, mimickery and quite often role play. For example, when one of our teachers became engaged, a mock wedding was preformed – father of the bride, brides-maids, best man, the lot! And here were the children of Scoil Ailbhe convinced that their teachers were all sane and sensible! So much for the secret lives of teachers, S.N.As, caretakers and so forth!

Scoil Ailbhe staff on Fancy Dress day - and all these were paid a salary!

Through the chair, please

My first real experience of the Irish National Teach ers Organisation (I.N.T.O.) was when I was encouraged by a senior teacher in Scoil Ailbhe – the late Willie O'Dwyer - to attend a union meeting. The experience must have struck a chord with me because from that moment I was captivated. As I write, in the height of a severe recession, trade unionism has come in for some serious bashing in certain quarters. Perhaps some people reading this chapter have their own opinions on these matters as of course is their right.

From my perspective, I can sincerely say that while the I.N.T.O. has always, and will continue to strive to improve the pay and conditions of its members – it also has had a huge input into securing improved and better services in education for the primary children of this state. This has been the case dating back to its foundation in 1868. A very vibrant Education Committee of the I.N.T.O. has consistently sought reform in Curricular areas and has regularly designed and delivered imaginative and modern inservice courses for teachers. It has also extracted much needed reforms in primary education from the Department of Education.

While the I.N.T.O. has very supportive members, it is true to say that about 20% take on an active role in the organisation. This would be on a par, I imagine with the administration of other bodies such as political parties, G.A.A. clubs, musical societies, golf clubs etc.

Over the years I have found the I.N.T.O. to be of enormous assistance to me during my teaching career. This was particularly so during my term as Principal. All one

All in favour please show!

had to do when seeking clarification on any educational/ administrative issue was to ring up Head Office for guid ance or advice and the information you sought was with you before close of business that very same day. I suppose, because of my involvement with the Organisation quite of- ten other teachers would make contact with me hoping that I might know something that they hadn't heard – which may or may not indeed be the case.

In rehearsing questions for interview for the Princi- palship I was asked on one or two occasions did I think ac- tive trade union membership would be in conflict with that role. Nothing could be further from the truth. Rather than it being an obstacle, on the contrary it was a serious help.

I.N.T.O. Annual Conferences were always fascinat- ing for me. To the best of my knowledge, I attended 32 in all. Locations varied from Kerry to Galway, Clare, Done- gal, Waterford, Wexford, Kilkenny, Limerick and Belfast. It was quite frequent and common for some media reports of same to chase minority news items at such Congresses: "Teachers jostle Minister" or "Teachers walk out on Min ister" and so on. 800 delegates would be present. 10 may walk out once every ten years. Does that 10 represent the I.N.T.O.? No. Do they represent 1% or 2%?. Yes. There are some young radicals in every Trade Union, Political party etc. year in year out. Invariably some of them go on to lead their organisation with the passing of time. A case of poacher becoming gamekeeper. Such is life.

In our own Thurles Branch I was glad to have been entrusted the chair for a term way back in the 80's. For about 10 years from 1987 onwards, Media Co-Ordinator for Mid Tipperary was a role I very much relished. District Xl denotes the area covered by Waterford, Tipperary and Clare. It was my honour and great privilege – to have chaired that District Committee Xl from 1992 to 1995. I was not a Principal then and looking back I would have liked to have been more familiar with Principals' issues in that role. I'm thinking here of Department Circulars, Department Grants and other relevant administrative issues.

I.N.T.O. President Declan Kelleher answers pupils' questions

I was also privileged to have acted as both Convener and Chairperson of North Tipperary Principals' Forum for a number of years.

While Principal, it gave me a great sense of satisfaction to have welcomed and received three I.N.T.O. Presidents to our school - Mr. Tony Bates for National Tree Week in 1997, Mr. Gerry Malone to open our new Computer Room in 2002 and more recently Mr. Declan Kelleher to open a New Resource Room in 2008.

Right now, Thurles is served by a very vibrant I.N.T.O. Branch with highly efficient officers. The logo on the Organisation's crest says "Serving Education" and if the usual suspects who write in some newspapers will forgive me, I believe it is very apt.

Before I complete this chapter, it would be remiss of me not to refer to the Irish Primary Principal's Network (I.P.P.N.) for its support is clearly manifested in the coming together locally, on a regular basis, of a small group of Principals, to discuss items of common interest. The I.P.P.N. facilitates and finances these support groups. It ultimately is to the benefit of Principals, schools and children alike.

Staff and Leadership

There have been countless pages written on leadership both within and outside of the education field. A warning quite frequently uttered by experts tells us that a good teacher may not necessarily make a good Principal but a poor teacher will certainly never become an efficient Principal.

I had started this chapter with the sole purpose of examining what are the attributes I have come to admire in a successful, talented, motivated, creative and efficient staff. On reflection though, I decided that I would approach that topic from another angle and rather analyse the qualities that every leader/Principal should place at the top of his/her aspiration list. I hasten to add, that I am not saying that I ticked all the boxes in the list to follow or indeed even the majority of them. What I will say, though, is that any leader/manager/Principal starting out as such, should aspire to them if they wish to gain success and excellence never mind fulfilment and contentment from their employees, staff, players or whatever :

- Trust people until you have reason not to.
- Don't ask somebody to do something you are not prepared to do yourself.
- Think before you speak. (As the saying goes, "Don't put your mouth into motion before your brain is in gear!")
- Keep strong communication lines open
- If someone makes a mistake, usually they know it only too well themselves. If a footballer sends a penalty wide there is no need to run in and shout, "You should have placed it to his left"
- If you make a mistake, no point in reflecting on it – as they say in hurling it's the next ball that counts.
- If you need to speak to a staff member about an issue, speak to

them on their own.

- Be prepared to listen.
- Acknowledge achievement.
- Reassure, give credit and encourage initiative.
- Be optimistic – if you support Leeds United you probably have learned that art already!
- Be as democratic as is reasonable. You can be too democratic, in which case it is well to remember that when significant decisions are reached, you are the person who will have to defend and justify them and, significantly, carry them through and, crucially, implement them.
- Don't be afraid to say, "No" – it has only one letter less than "Yes". Keep saying, "Yes" to everything and everybody and see where it gets you!!
- Be consistent.
- Treat everybody equally and fairly.
- Promote a sense of fun.
- Be supportive of people who act in the best interests of others.
- Use common sense… of course what one person considers to be common sense might not necessarily receive support from another… but be that as it may, still use common sense!
- Empathise to the best of your ability.
- Be available.
- Be visible.
- Facilitate sensible, innovative ideas.
- Follow through on decisions.
- Keep calm.
- If you are still alive after all that, congratulate yourself.

How many of these ideals did I live up to – well you would have to ask my staff about that wouldn't you? All I can say is that I hope I met some of them and that arising from that, that they would have got some reasons to respond appropriately. Incidentally, since my own very early days, an early morning browse through the day's newspaper was the perfect start to the challenges ahead. I have often placed it on record in newsletters, at parents' meetings, at concerts or wherever that I was always exceptionally proud of my staff and would have considered them to be talented, progressive, creative, highly motivated, obliging, open, co-operative and seriously professional people. The fact that I was involved with others in the appointing of 80% of them or so I would have taken great satisfaction on seeing, not just how they fulfilled the promise shown on appointment but also how their friendship and teamwork developed as the years progressed. Consequently, the real winners ultimately are the children.

It would be remiss of me if I failed to mention and indeed acknowledge the significant contribution which the female members in the staff have made to what is an all boys school. Recent research in the U.S.A. tells us of the qualities sisters can bring to a family – it speaks of a caring, concerned and responsible approach they bring to the table, so to speak. I would readily concur with that thinking, as it relates to school. Of course, the male members bring another dimension of their own to proceedings. All in all, a good gender mix is a major plus both in the school and indeed in the staffroom. I would go further and state that a mixing of genders among pupils is the more sensible and progressive way to educate. There are many young people in single sex schools who reach third level education not being at ease at relating to the opposite sex – all the more so if they have no siblings of a different gender. I have no doubt there are many people who would hold a different view on a topic which is always good for a lively debate.

No account of staff relations would be complete without referring to the essential element of a sense of fun among the group. There can be no doubt but that young teachers (and staff) help to make sure that more senior staff members remain young at heart. Nobody took themselves too seriously in our school, but if they had any notions in that direction, rest assured they would be swiftly discouraged. Good humour and general banter were never too far away in our staff room. They were a commodity that contributed enormously to a school with "atmosphere". At least this was the word often used by visitors to our seat of learning – an observation that was very flattering indeed. I have referred to the "staff" here as often as it occurs to me to use that word. Not too long ago staff meant "teachers". Nowadays of course, there is a much more inclusive meaning to the term, with the appointment of Special Needs Assistants (S.N.A.s), caretakers and secretaries (albeit in many cases regrettably only on a part time basis – if at all) to our schools.

I spoke earlier of the attributes that staff would hope to expect from their leader. I will conclude by listing a few that a leader might hope for in his/her staff:

- Dedication, professionalism and good organisational skills.
- Good communication and initiative.
- Not pushing the boundaries.
- Sticking to deadlines (note the word "dead" as part of that word!).
- Being a teamplayer.
- An ability to think outside the box.

I would be very confident that any reader here could add many more of their own.

Past Pupils Reminiscing

The memories of past pupils, not surprisingly, are as varied as the types of car that they drive. Many can recall events from their school days as vividly as if it was only weeks ago. Others, while intrigued by the notion of nostalgia, readily admit that all that time in their lives is somewhat of a blur. Some with the former tendency relish an opportunity to regale you with commendable detail of those times while others are at their very embellishing best near the midnight hour, assisted by a number of stimulating beverages in some local tavern. They may not be too forthcoming in a more formal setting but in the right environment they come into their own.

At different intervals I have been reminded of many schoolday gems, many recalled to me since retirement. Excuses that sound original have always fascinated children and indeed, if they were to admit it, teachers likewise. A former pupil of the school reminds me of a morning from another era when he was quite late for school. His usual mode of transport was a donkey and cart driven the mile or so into town by his father. On this particular morning, as the clock ticked towards ten o'clock, he rushed breathlessly in the classroom door to offer the excuse, "I couldn't catch the ass, Sir". As would be expected, the excuse nearly brought the house down.

These were the days when kettles were unable to switch themselves off but rather sputtered and bobbled until the plug was detached from the socket. It was common enough to have quite a number of country kids attending our establishment. I can easily recall one such child, who had a very cultured accent, arriving late into my class one morning to offer a very genuine excuse (but nonetheless, one which amused his classmates) saying that, "The cawlves (calves) broke out, sir." Of course, most people would be familiar with, "The wind was against me, sir," uttered by a thoughtful cyclist only for some boy arriving from the opposite direction a few minutes later with the same excuse! I have been informed of a boy who arrived late after dinner (in the days when boys went home for dinner) to offer the reason for delay as because, "The meat was tough, sir."

Of course, there were also the classic excuses of the most unoriginal type. Top of the list here would be, "It's in the wash, sir." This, in response to, "Where is your uniform/tracksuit/tie/shirt/pants, John?" This was definitely in "The dog ate my homework" category. As mentioned briefly elsewhere in this book "the mother" excuse was wheeled out with monotonous regularity. "Where is your homework, Joe?" "Sir, my mother …" "Have you the money for the swimming, Tom?" "Sir, my mother …" "Did you bring back the form, Kevin?" "Sir, my mother…." and so on. I often wonder do the mothers of this nation know at all how much they are responsible for all the foibles of their offsprings!!

Many of the past pupils' memories have to do with physical aspects of their school i.e. polished floors, long corridors (at least twice as short now that they have become adults) vast staircases, rows of coat hangers forever imprinted in their minds as dragon-like figures. More re call the slides they made on the ice in the schoolyard, all the better if somebody sneaked some water onto it. The melodious tuning fork was associated by some with choir masters or choir mistresses of the day. This little device would be unfamiliar to to-day's children, with a range of musical instruments at their disposal to help them find the required key. The old school bell held a fascination for many of a certain vintage. In later times of course this historic piece of equipment has been replaced by the buzzer. Those boys, who held the honour of being responsible for ringing the bell from an upstairs window, consider themselves to have contributed considerably to the organisation of the school, as it was then, and so they have. One of our teachers recalls a bellringer rushing downstairs after short break one morning to tell him, "The bell is gone, sir". To which the teacher replied "I know, sure I heard it." "No, sir," came the reply "but the bell is really gone". After much effort at clarification by both sides it transpired that as the bellringer was ringing the bell out a window leading from the top corridor, that the actual gong from the bell had fallen off and landed among the playing children in the yard below!

Nearly every boy has a memory of eating sweets in class while the teacher was teaching and certainly every teacher has a distinct memory of it too! In the early years I wondered why a boy would approach to report, "Sir, Jack has sweets under his desk". However, one day the penny dropped. "And did you ask him for one?" "I did, Sir". "And did he give you one?" "No, Sir". "So you said you'd tell on him?" "Yes, Sir". (sheepishly). Blackmail was alive and well in Scoil Ailbhe!

Some former pupils have reminded me of the gentleness of the late Most Rev. Dr. Morris, the Archbishop of Cashel and Emly. They remember him visiting the classroom to examine them for Confirmation. So do I. A favourite and very relevant question of his was, "And tell me now, how would you bear witness to Jesus in Ard na Croise or Loughtagalla or Clongour?"

Others still recall schools' cross country days of mud, rain, umbrellas, spikes, loudhailers, sandwiches, medals, parental encouragement and the odd fanatic roaring, "Will you go up for Tommy O'Riordan's medal or are you deaf?" Memories too abound of the exciting task of being asked to remove the blackboard duster to the yard for the purpose of cleaning off the excessive chalk dust. Many recall the irregular duster prints on the back of the bicycle shed. One boy told me his favourite task was monitoring the rain gauge which had been secured in an area of the school's front lawn. The Brother was sometimes baffled by the readings, however, not knowing that Damien made a habit of drinking the water. A story somewhat similar was told of two boys who were sent out to the staff room to make a cup of tea for their teacher. (Health and Safety must have been in its infancy!) On returning, the teacher took a sip but immediately spat it out with a disdainful grin. "The problem was," regaled Barry afterwards, "we forgot to boil the kettle!"

Other accounts tell us of memorable school tours to Tramore, Callan (the home of the founder of the Christian Brothers, Edmund Ignatius Rice), The Burren, Bray, Dublin and so on while more still rate their experiences singing in Cór na nÓg with their colleagues as memorable for a number of reasons – usually for the enjoyment gained, the thrill of meeting up with the girls, the performance in the National Concert Hall or for a small minority the boredom of it all!

Thomas remembers the sheer embarrassment of coming up to Scoil Ailbhe or "The Brothers" (as it was often called) from the Presentation Convent School and his mother of 40 years beside him and "she having grey hairs on her head". He kept telling her, "Go on away now

Mammy I'm alright", in case "Murphy and Hayes would see her and I'd be mortified!" The same boy recalls on leaving primary school in the late sixties that his standard of Irish was on a par with that of Honours Inter Cert (as it was then).

As mentioned elsewhere, the event that is recalled with unparalleled fondness is always the school's Christmas Concert – lines fluffed, crazy costumes, the mystique of a school's interior after dark and of course the games and diversion in the classroom while waiting to go on or after the performance was over. Whether they were aware of it or not (or cared), the classroom supervision amid the unprecedented hype was the one aspect of the concert that tested teachers' patience well into the night.

Matters religious remained with some. They can vividly remember a decade of the Rosary around the grotto during the month of May with the whole school lined up in both corridors to recite the prayer if the day was wet. Many took part in May Processions – reluctantly, or otherwise – and Corpus Christi processions when traffic was less and devotion was more.

Former pupils recall with pride colleagues and classmates who went on to make a name for themselves be it in sport, show business, politics or whatever. They are proud to relate the deeds of Scoil Ailbhe men who performed heroically for the Tipperary senior hurlers. Among those they mention would be: Jimmy Doyle, Paul Byrne, Jimmy Duggan, Michael Murphy, Francis Murphy, T.J. Semple, Michael Doyle, Eddie and Johnny Enright, Brendan Carroll, Tom Barry, Ger "Redser" O'Grady, Pa Bourke, Pádraic Maher and the hat trick hero of the 2010 All-Ireland, Lar Corbett. International athletes Tommy Moloney and Bill Mullaney are also remembered.

Comedian, Pat Shortt, tells us that he recalls playing one of the Three Wise Men in the school's Christmas Concert and thinks that he never played a wise man since!

The Singing Doctor, Ronan Tynan pays tribute to the late Fintan Brennan for encouraging his unique tenor voice, recalling Fintan's delight when he, Ronan, sang "Oh Holy Night" one Christmas.

Other former pupils of the school like to remind us that they were in the same class as pianist, Frank McNamara of R.T.E. fame. Others still recall Louth T.D. Fergus O'Dowd when he attended. I had the pleasure, myself, of taking past pupil Richard Quirke of Dr. Quirkey's Good Time Emporium around the school one Saturday morning, something which he assured me he thoroughly enjoyed, re newing as it did, once again, his childhood experiences in his alma mater.

Finally, a boast I hear from one of my daughters now and again, is that she was on the Presentation Quiz team (in a Pioneer Quiz) which defeated a corresponding team from Scoil Ailbhe which featured the Irish Independent's Political Editor, Fionnán Sheahan! I'm sure he can live with that.

Children mirror society

Working with children can be very rewarding. One should never underestimate their potential for achievement, creativity, entertainment, discovery, thoughtfulness, empathy, acquiring knowledge and information, good manners, respect, Christianity and much more. Unfortunately human nature being what it is, the opposite is also the case. Every time I read about or become aware from television or radio that a person has achieved greatness, wealth or good fortune in some sphere or other a particular thought occurs to me. The very same thought enters my mind when I learn of somebody hitting the headlines through infamy – be it through involvement in crime, being locked up in prison or whatever. The thought being that that person once attended a primary school. We cannot say for sure that s/he ever attended a secondary school, a vocational school, a community or comprehensive school or a third level college, but we can always say with near certainty that s/he went through the primary system. So, you might ask, the point being?

Well the point being that when one considers the wide range of children who attend our first level system, bearing in mind levels of ability, background etc., the mystery is that the final outcome is largely successful. After all we have gifted children with extremely high I.Q's to children at the other extreme of intellectual ability, children of different levels of language capacity, financial advantage, attendance record, social skills all attending together. Throw into the equation all the well known factors that determine progress such as affluence, poverty, deprivation, home environment, special needs, security, self esteem, being loved and cared for, common sense and, of course, health and the degree of our success is indeed remarkable.

Thankfully, many children sail through their primary school experience with little problems. Side by side with those are a minority of troubled children. Many of these pupils have experienced a traumatic experience and may still be experiencing the same. Neglect can be the most common factor here, be it through lack of attention, care, supervision, security, love and reassurance. These children may also suffer from hunger or from illness and are often the victims of violence, abuse or addiction. I believe it is important that I place on record that my experience of the H.S.E.'s Social Work Department's input into Child Protection in this region has been very positive.

In the area of Special Needs Education, the progress made in the last decade or more has been revolutionary. The sanctioning of Resource Teachers to this area has been hugely significant for many reasons, not least being their expertise in developing the social skills and self esteem of such children. The appointment of Special Needs Assistants was another development which has become invaluable to this progress. Language Support for immigrant children heralded a welcome dimension to primary school but unfortunately cutbacks have greatly interfered with the service. Services such as the National Psychological Service (N.E.P.S.) and the Speech and Language Therapy Services, while an improvement on what was available in that area at the turn of the century, still leave much to be desired due to a lack of funding and personnel.

From time to time a pupil will refuse point blank to come to school. I have often encountered a boy in a distressed state at the door of the school accompanied by an exasperated parent. Often the parent will say they just don't know why this is so. They wonder could there be a bullying problem, could it be about homework, could it be an issue with the teacher etc.

One can never rule out any of those reasons of course and they are worth investigating. However, it is my experience that the most time this refusal occurs is when one parent has left the home – be it through extended leave abroad, bereavement, separation or any other such reason. The child, consequently, is reluctant to leave the remaining parent, worried that when he returns home that that parent may be missing also. This should never be a reason for the parent to feel guilty – rather is it essential that parents should understand why this behaviour is happening and to talk it through with their child. Every effort should be made to insist that the child comes in to the school, otherwise it will be twice as difficult the next morning.

Troublesome, disruptive pupils present one of the biggest challenges to any teacher. Sometimes there is a misguided perception there that this is not a problem at primary level, "Sure they are all too young and innocent" and so on. This observation or theory, alas, is often wide of the mark. After all criminals and thugs didn't all of a sudden start acting up when they became teenagers! Unfortunately, there are not many raised eyebrows among primary teachers when confronted by some stark headline on law breaking from that week's court reports in the local newspaper.

Children are no different to adults in that they thrive on orderly situations. They respond to order and organisation and flourish by it. On occasion, when this is lacking and discipline is loose, trouble will emerge. This can sometimes occur through inexperience on a teacher's part, or perhaps on occasion a qualified teacher is unavailable for substitution purposes. It is vital that every young teacher starting out should have survival as their motto. They have to show with certainty at the outset who is in charge and, more importantly, who will continue to be in charge. This would have been preached regularly in the Colleges of Education but it is only in the heat of battle that they can confirm that they are worthy soldiers.

Experienced teachers also would be foolhardy to think that they were prepared for every situation as I found out one day about 20 years ago. Every Tuesday morning at that time two boys used to call to each classroom selling Saving Stamps for the School's Saving Scheme. There could be six or eight boys who would have money to buy some. So rather than allowing the transaction to be a distraction while I taught, I used to ask the six or eight boys to conduct their business outside the door in the corridor. For some strange reason, on this particular day, I asked the boys to show me their stamps as they returned to the room. One boy (we'll call him Robert) arrived in last. So I said,

" Can I see your stamps Robert?
"Ah.... I don't have any sir"
"Oh! Why not?"
"I don't know sir"
"And why did you go out then?"
"For the mess sir"

At that stage one of the boys piped up and said, "Sir he's going out there every Monday for the last five or six weeks." I can tell you for the rest of the time while that system of selling stamps was in place – and that wasn't very long – I made sure I took a leaf out of the Customs Officers' book by asking, "Anything to declare" as the boys returned to the classroom. The moral is pretty obvious – one can learn something new at any stage of one's career!

Quick sales, tall tales and junk mails

In keeping with many other organisations (I presume) schools are bombarded on an ongoing basis by unscheduled visits from salespeople, vigorous commercialism, endless competitions and meaningless junk mail. Were schools profit making businesses, perhaps our toleration levels for some of the above maybe somewhat higher. As we are not in the retail business, or involved in a profit making service, most Principals of my acquaintance consider sales, promotions etc. an unnecessary intrusion on their day. Furthermore, it is scarcely necessary to record here that excess (or indeed sufficient) money in a primary school is as common as tips in a Thurles chipper.

We are often told that one of the many indicators of communication is body language. When approached by an enthusiastic salesperson for some inconsequential gadget – not having made a prior appointment - I'm afraid I haven't always come up to the mark! As Scoil Ailbhe was in the middle of the town, perhaps we were blessed with more callers that more isolated schools. Sensible teaching Principals, of course, cannot afford to be so interrupted as naturally their number one priority lies in the teaching of their pupils. Our school, and others like it, having got an administrative Principal may give the impression that, once the crossword was complete, the second newspaper put to bed and the third cup of coffee down the hatch we were now ready to be entertained for an hour or two! And Yes, I have also been told, "Ah sure, they have to make a living too" No doubt, but scarcely out of shoe string schools.

A short time ago a play was being staged in the local Source Theatre. It was called "Death of a Salesman". Some of my staff mischievously enquired if I was the author!

I must, in all fairness, record here that a very small minority made prior appointments and that, furthermore, representatives from well known schools' publishing companies – who had a product of relevance – were always very courteous and, I feel, got a fair hearing. Otherwise, the following little exchange might be typical now and again.

Sales Rep : (knocks on an open door) –
Flan isn't it?

F.Q. (In the middle of compiling the annual sta
tistics for the Dept of Ed)
Yes (thinking, 'of course it's Flan. You met the
postman on the way in')

S.R. My name's Shane.
There aren't too many Quigleys in this area

F.Q. (thinking 'now you're gone from the frying
pan into the fire') No. It's
Quigney. QUIG – NEE

S.R. Oh! That's an unusual one. (looks around at
all the hurleys and helmets in the corner of the
office.) How will ye do in the hurling Sunday?

F.Q. Who?

S.R. Tipp. They're playing Clare aren't they?

F.Q. (Thinking 'Unfortunately') Ah! A draw
I'd say (thinking 'This Conversation is going no
where'). Was I expecting you?

S. R. Not really. I was in the area and I just
thought I'd drop in. (Opening Briefcase) I was
wondering would you be interested in this new
product our company, Wishy Washy has on the

market? It's out on its own for stain removing.
Can I take you down the corridor to the …
F.Q. No thanks. I'm not interested really.
S.R. Are you sure now. I can…
F.Q. No thanks we have no money. I'm pretty
busy at the moment and besides I'm afraid you
have   not made an appointment. O.K. Thank you
now. Good luck (Exit Shane)

At times like this I have often wondered could you
see your doctor, dentist, solicitor, accountant, hairdresser,
architect, hotel manager, bank manager, swimming instructor, driving instructor etc. without an appointment.

Salespitching through children is not a new concept. There is a constant effort made by numerous companies to advertise their products with parents, through
schoolchildren. It is every Principal's duty and responsibility to resist this exploitative attempt to target children, or
through them, to target their parents. Promotions by various companies urging the collection of tokens by parents
are a perfect example of this form of marketing. Parents
are challenged sufficiently at home on their own doorsteps
and at their own letterboxes than to have to face an extra
barrage coming from their school.

I have always likened my role, in this area, to that
of a good full back – keep the ball out of the square and
protect your goalie!

Competing strongly for the same market are hordes
of charities, all seemingly good causes. Again, parents have
their own favourite charities to subscribe to at home, in the
street or at the church gate. That is quite adequate I'm sure.
Our policy in our school has been that we would do our bit
for a chosen four or five charities – mostly local – and after

that we would have considered that we had played our part.

When it comes to competitions – everybody has a bright idea. It is safe to assume that you could be entering one type of competition or another every day of every school year. There seems to be a kind of mindset in some organisations "How will we get publicity for such and such? Ah sure what about running a competition in the primary school?" From time to time a phone call will reach us. "Hello, this is Lisa here from Universal Solutions. We sent you a flyer there last week on our new initiative/prod uct/competition. We were wondering if you received it." At that moment you are thinking, "I wonder which one of those 37 items of junk mail, that arrived within the last month would that be?" Of course the requirement to be polite takes over and you do not tell her that it is already in the bin. I often think junk mail producers must be a God send for the Waste Paper recycling industry. A stream of nourishment for the Red Bin.

The Planning and Building Unit of the Department of Education is based in Tullamore. This is where schools apply for Grant aid for numerous structural improvements including Summer Work Schemes. To be perfectly fair to the said Department we secured a satisfactory level of assistance from them over my years as Principal – New school furniture, school yards resurfaced, re-wiring of school, installation of a lift, replacement of Central Heating Boiler and so on. As could be expected a serious degree of paperwork was involved with all applications for financial as sistance and particularly so with Summer Work Schemes. Coupled with administration, a consistent level of tenacity was also required. However, when the end result justified the means a great level of satisfaction was derived by the instigator.

Imagine then when you receive a letter from one (or two) of our public representatives informing you that they have just received a letter from the Minister (copy included) which reads something like this:

Dear Mr./ Mrs. Whoever, T.D.,
    I was delighted to have received representations from you on behalf of Scoil Ailbhe, Thurles, with regard to the installation of a new lift at the school.
    I am pleased to inform you that the application has been successful. If I can be of any further assistance in this matter please do not hesitate to contact me.

Mise le meas,
Mr. /Mrs. Whathisorhername, T.D.,
Minister for Education & Skills,
Dáil Eireann.

Interestingly the previous Monday when you rang the Department they had no account of when a decision would be forthcoming. (This, in effect meant they weren't allowed to say until the Minister issued his epistle to his/ her supporting T.D.). So now the T.D. has delivered! Or has s/he? A phone call usually comes from the T.D.'s office also to confirm the goods news. How nice ! How obliging is our local T.D.! But wait a minute. How did s/he know we had applied for funding for the lift, boiler, windows, doors, Summer Work Scheme or whatever? Of course s/he didn't. But a little game has to be played between the Minister and the T.D. Too bad if you have been slaving away at your application over the last few months, doing the donkey work yourself and getting the job done by the Modh Díreach without favour from anybody. Oh! The hypocracy of it!

Does somebody think somebody is being fooled by this little exercise in timewasting, resource wasting and money wasting?

So to conclude a chapter that has a "Talk to Joe" element about it, I will include a few common phrases which make frequent appearances on flyers of one kind or another and to which I have a distinct allergy:

Are ye winding down? (In the month of June when you were never as busy!)

It's that time of year again… (Can we be a little more original?)

We sincerely hope you are refreshed again after the holidays and have the batteries charged….(Yes, I have got an introduction like that sent to me yesterday already…and the day before… and ..)

I know this is a very busy time of year for you… but…(But you still want X,Y and Z)

The match/meeting/programme etc. will take place @ 12 a.m./12 p.m.

This latter piece with the 12 a.m./12 p.m. first came to my attention on Sky T.V. and has come into frequent use in recent times.

Now, when I studied Latin in secondary school all those years ago I learned that p.m. stood for post meridiem (after midday). So how could 12 noon be 12 p.m. as it is not yet after midday? 12.01 p.m. yes but 12 p.m., no. Similarly with a.m. meaning ante meridiem (before midday), 12 at night should read 12 midnight – not 12 a.m. Now that that's off my chest I think I can return to my crossword.

Tricks of the Trade

Strange how a little lesson learned in the very early years teaching springs back into your consciousness in later years. There is no apparent reason for this, no more than a sudden reminder of an old acquaintance of some forty years standing. I wonder if every new teacher experiences a similar delusion. I refer here to an occasion when you are teaching a slightly complicated part of a lesson, let us say the rotation of the earth around the sun. You come to a tricky stage in your explanation of the principle. You are not too sure yourself! However you plough ahead deluding yourself that "Ah sure even if I'm not too clear on this part myself, sure there is every chance some of the lads will get it anyway." A curiosity of mine to this day is did other novice teachers ever fool themselves with such a nonsensical theory? A few months into the job were sufficient to banish any such delusion. Reality dawned, and it soon became as clear as a desert sky that if you didn't understand the material you were teaching yourself, there was no chance that your pupils would! Nonetheless, sometimes outside of the school environment, when I hear somebody making a public pronouncement on some issue to an audience, I fleetingly ponder, "I wonder does s/he understand what s/he is saying him/herself"!

Another home truth that makes an impression on you in the earlier stages of teaching is the futility of reading some information to children rather than presenting it or teaching it to them. Pause from actually teaching the topic for a few minutes, any experienced teacher will tell you, and start reading information for a short period and you can fold up your tent. You have lost them. We are often told that unless data is interesting, or interestingly presented, the recipient will lose concentration after about twenty seconds. Is it any wonder we see people nodding off in public places while somebody reads at them – and I'm not talking about bedtime stories! Stories, of course, are a different matter – but still are much better when presented properly. I often wonder when I listen to speeches, sermons and lectures being read out monotonously how productive is the exercise at all. Many of them remind me of the Queen's speech on Christmas Day or Robert Emmet's Speech from the Dock. My advice would simply be, try that style out in a classroom for a while and see will you need security if repeated! Would they climb the walls? Would they knock the walls?

It is pretty obvious from what I have written above that teaching, no more than any other career, is a learning curve. So what else have I learned over the years?

Well I have learned, what any experienced parent will know, that when a child is pretty agitated and distressed that a cooling off period is vital. From time to time a dust up of some considerable ferocity will erupt between a couple of pupils in the school playground. In the past, I have often heard responsible teachers raising their voices, often in staccato fashion giving the interviewee little time to contribute. I have no doubt that I was guilty of that interrogation style in other times also. Life, however, teaches us that intense interrogation in the immediate aftermath of a serious conflict is not very productive. Quite often when such offenders were sent to my office I would ask them to take a seat in the reception area, that I was looking after other matters at the moment (not always true) and that I would talk to them when I was ready. In the meantime, I would engross myself in some other business and return to efforts at reconciliation when temperatures had cooled. The prospects for reason to return to all sides had usually increased and the likelihood of progressive concessions was brighter.

There were times when, as a class teacher, some misdemeanour by an individual pupil would have been deemed to be the last straw and I'd had enough. A stern directive would go out to the culprit to take himself straight to the Principal's office. On his return I would ask the offending boy "Well what did Bro. such and such say?" "He said to apologise and not to do it again", might be the reply. My immediate reaction would have been, to think, "Is that the best he could manage?"

When roles became reversed and I was in the Principal's office and a similar situation arose I saw things from a different angle. I now had the view that the very fact that the boy had been sent to my office was sufficiently serious in itself and was adequate punishment – for most pupils – together with a stern warning of course. I always made it my business to explain this line to staff members lest there be a misunderstanding of positions.

There were, of course, times when repeat offenders frequented my office. Other approaches and remedies had then to be explored. The most common excuse trotted out by a pupil in trouble is, "I was only messing, Sir". "Messing" has a broad meaning for teachers. The following definitions have revealed themselves to me over a 45 year period. The word "messing" in my dictionary could be described thus:

Messing: part of a verb meaning grinning, jeering, joking, smiling, smirking, name calling, teasing, slapping, punching, boxing, kicking, head butting.

Of course, the obvious answer to a disclosure of

messing is that it is only messing if both parties consider it to be so. The occasional pupil in trouble, in an attempt to win favour, will try his hand at diversion – a very common feature in every classroom. I well recall a boy, who had come to our school from a smaller establishment in another part of the country, saying to me, "Sir, in the last school I was in, the Principal was a teacher". This was a view very common among many children, that if you weren't actually teaching a class, well then you weren't a teacher at all!

I suppose a piece of advice many teachers could keep to the forefront of their wisdom banks – and indeed many parents too – is that once a child has been reprimand-ed and a significant point is made, that the lecture should end there. Much research has told us that after a period of less than half a minute of correction etc. the human mind switches off and the shutters are erected. I will readily con-fess that I have to issue a plea of guilty here on occasion in the past.

This might be just as good a time as any to apolo gise to Jimmy a lovely pupil who was part of my second class in my second year in Thurles. The flame haired pupil was but twenty minutes, I would say, in my class one July day in 1967 when I called him up to receive a slap! His offence? Talking to the seven year old pupil beside him! This surely was an act of an insecure young teacher, over intent on laying down the law early. They say tact is the art of making a point without making an enemy. Well this, while a country mile from tact could easily (temporarily or otherwise) have made an instant enemy.

Almost 40 years later I met up with the same genial Jimmy and offered a sincere apology to him for my un-warranted petulance. He was as gracious as I would have expected, "I never remember that, put it out of your mind, the only memories I had from your class were good ones, etc. etc." His sentiments were both magnanimous and reassuring. Why does one incident, albeit from a different era, stand out in an ageing memory? Guilt I presume. Thankfully, forgiveness is a rich commodity among us. Past pupils, I've no doubt, for the most part concur with the saying that love blinds us to faults, but hatred blinds us to virtues. Hopefully they do anyway!

Memorable Visitors

The first Newsletter I sent home as Principal to parents was being read by our then Chairperson of the Board of Management, Fr. Eugene one day. He suggested that I should file away all such Newsletters which would in time, form a record of events in the school as they happened. I thought it to be an inspired idea and consequently, all Newsletters over the last thirteen years have now contrived to form something of a historical record of that period. No doubt, other schools in various parts already do something similar. I found it particularly useful as an information aid for newly appointed teachers. From it, they would have seen the sequence – and the nature – of events as they happened during the course of the school year.

Glancing through the collection, hidden here and there among various newsitems, are a few little events that in some ways stand out from the rest. Pretty unique indeed, was the visit of President Mary McAleese to our school

President Mary McAleese visits Scoil Ailbhe

Minister for Education, Mary Hanafin T.D. makes a point, 2006.

in June 2003; a memorable visit from an exceptional lady. Making a return to her native town in March 2006 was the then Minister for Education Mary Hanafin T.D. who honoured us with her presence. Her familiarity with children and the classroom was clearly evident from the moment she set foot in Scoil Ailbhe.

There were special days when Irish Rugby star Alan Quinlan and former G.A.A. President Seán McCague graced us with their presence. Seán and myself attended St. Pat's at the same time. One member of our staff quipped as Seán entered the building with me, "One of these men went on to distinguish himself. .and the other became President of the G.A.A.!"

Whole School Evaluations (W.S.E.s) took place over this period – always occasions that, to put it mildly, cause a stir. This is when a number of Inspectors spend a few days in the school evaluating progress, efficiency etc. They are occasions when a lot of paperwork is required, but the bottom line here always is that when people are go-

Patrick and Brian proudly display the Heineken Cup

ing about their work honestly, there is, and should not be, anything to fear.

Always an exciting day in any school is when victorious teams come to meet the boys. Eyes pop, adrenalin rises and every vantage point is taken – and those are only the staff! During my time there 4 McCarthy Cups arrived – 1971, 1989, 1991 and 2001. 3 County Senior Champion teams from Thurles Sarsfields visited – 1974, 2005 and 2009. The Heineken Cup made two appearances (did I say Thurles was in Munster?!) recently. Of course, numerous other victorious teams from the town appeared including The Harty Cup and Croke Cup winners of 2009, our friends from Thurles C.B.S.

A name that keeps regularly cropping up in our Newsletters was that of our exceptional librarian and sup-

Ireland & Munster star, Alan Quinlan visits

President of the I.N.T.O. Mr. Gerry Malone, cuts the tape to perform the opening of Scoil Ailbhe's new computer room in 2002

porter, Eve. This lady criss-crosses the country once a week to provide the pupils with an unrivalled library service.

Finally, prominent among the later entries is an account of the equipping of all classrooms with Interactive Whiteboards and the establishing of a comprehensive Music Programme throughout the school – on a phased basis – together with a new Music Room – all made possible through the great generosity and support of the people of Thurles and the surrounding area together with sponsorship from one particularly generous past pupil.

G.A.A. President, Sean McCague, with Bill McCormack

Chasing the dream

For the past fifteen years or so I have acted as an Independent Assessor on the Diocesan Panel. This is a list from which Independent Assessors are drawn to assist with the appointing of Primary Teachers, Special Needs Assistants, Caretakers and Secretaries. In each of these cases the Selection Board consists of three people – The Chairperson of the Board of Management, The Principal and an Independent Assessor drawn from the Diocesan Panel. When a Principal is being appointed, the Selection Board is made up of The Chairperson and two Independent Assessors. In all cases the Selection Board must reflect gender equity.

As you would imagine, most appointments relate to teachers. I can honestly say that the standard of applicants who present themselves for interview is extremely impressive. There is no doubt but that the calibre of young teachers who qualify – for the most part – is top class. It is very common to interview confident, articulate, talented and intelligent candidates.

Any time I interviewed in my own school I always regretted that there was normally only one job on offer. Frequently I would have wished that we could have chosen three or four.

Often people ask if I have any recommendations to help applicants with interviews. There are many pieces of advice I could give prospective candidates. I'm sure they have often been mentioned elsewhere and certainly they are far from being exhaustive. Anyway here's my tuppence worth:

- Present your C.V. neatly. An untidy C.V. may be an indication of general apathy.

- C.Vs should be to the point and not long winded. Basic information wins the day.
- If you require your C.V. returned (and who doesn't) please include a S.A.E. of A4 size. If the envelope is of the Motor Tax variety (in size) then it will be impossible to return all documents in such an envelope. In other words large means large.
- If you are nervous, it may be reassuring for you to know that I have quite often experienced Selection Board members who are also very nervous!
- When giving your answers remain interesting. How? Give the answers long enough to cover the question but short enough to hold the attention of the people interviewing you.
- Avoid long winded answers.
- Stick to the point. Don't ramble.
- Be honest. Don't bluff. Bluffing in fact, can be suspect ed fairly easily by those sitting across the table from you.
- Be yourself. Nobody else.
- All the advice about being courteous and well presented I take it as a given.
- Don't be afraid to ask a question or two when the interview is over. Write them down beforehand so that you won't forget.
- Be on time for the interview.

I have left the last piece of advice until last on purpose. Like any work in which you are involved for a considerable period one comes across funny incidents. However, the nature of this work is too confidential and serious for me to divulge any here, other than one which relates to being on time.

At one particular interview in which I participated, we got a phone call from a candidate to inform us that she had some difficulty finding the hotel and that she would be somewhat late. So we waited. And waited, until eventually the poor exhausted lady rushed in way behind time and most apologetic. During the course of the subsequent interview a member of the Selection Board asked the question, "Sinéad (we'll call her) what would you say was your greatest achievement to date?" To which Sinéad replied with a twinkle in her eye, "I suppose finding the hotel"

Now and then as an independent Assessor I would get a call from an unsuccessful candidate asking how they could improve for the next interview. Invariably it is the most impressive candidates that are curious. My answer generally would be to carry on as normal, on another day they could have been successful. It is often a mistake for somebody who is unsuccessful to start blaming themselves i.e. "If only I said this", or "I should have done that". More likely the reason could be (a) the sheer excellence of the person who secured the position (b) Timing – as in maybe the school was looking for expertise in music, sport, I.T., Drama, Art whatever. The next job might have different requirements (c) It could be that the successful person already was temporarily employed in the school and the Board etc. was thoroughly happy with them. That is no reflection on you so keep the chin up and focus even more determinedly on the next job.

Teachers and Teaching

So what makes an effective teacher? I'm sure one could write a full book on this topic alone. People often say "Oh I'd never make a teacher. I wouldn't have the patience." The implication there is that patience is the number one requirement. I know many people with patience but they may not necessarily make effective teachers.

My top requirement would be organisation. Other qualities would include good communication skills, being a team player, a certain degree of tolerance, a love of working with children, an ability to meet deadlines, patience, calmness under pressure, an ability to learn on the job and to upskill, consistency, fairness, a sense of fun, an ability to praise when due, a willingness to seek advice and last, but by no means least, a capacity to enforce a workable discipline. Any teacher already reading this is probably saying "Phew! He's not expecting much!" Well, indeed, perhaps no such perfect person exists but we can aspire to all the above and I know many teachers who go a long way towards ticking all those boxes.

Which takes me to criticism of teachers. There must be very few professions that receive so much flak. Reasons for why this is so, vary from a bad experience from a person's own school days to a perception that because children go home from school at 3 p.m. each day and get long holidays that teaching is a "soft" number, to the fact that because everybody went to school in their youth that they are now experts on how the job should be done. Take your pick. What is very obvious is that certain commentators in certain sections of the media consider criticism of teachers as being a bloodsport. These same people suitably ignore the myriad of tasks that teachers take on – on a daily basis – which are above and beyond the call of duty. During my career I have seen teachers returning to school weeks before the end of the Summer holidays to prepare for the new year, returning to school at night to upskill voluntarily in some area of the curriculum, fundraising for some education cause in the absence of Department of Education funding, attending quizzes by night, training teams during their lunch break and after school, attending Familiarisation Nights, Open Evenings, First Communion Ceremonies, week-end Confirmation Ceremonies, supervising children waiting for buses etc. and much more besides, and of course the after hours correction of homework.

Unwarranted, poorly researched and biased reporting on the profession can be quite demoralising for younger teachers in particular. As teachers grow older there is a more "Well that's their opinion, they're entitled to it I suppose" attitude. If it is a newspaper article we tend to see the heading, ignore the article and turn to the Sports pages or the Fashion page or whatever.

It has also to be acknowledged here and very forcefully, that there is a huge volume of support and admiration for the work of teachers out there among the vast silent majority. Having spent many evenings "on point duty" as the children exited at day's end, I am very well aware of that. Generally speaking, parents have a very positive attitude towards the work of teachers, place enormous value on it and are deeply appreciative of it – and the more often teachers hear that and know it the better.

Retirement

Have you any notion of retiring? The first time I was asked this question I was 43 and I nearly choked on my lucozade sport (or whatever the equivalent was at that time). As the years went by, a question something similar arose with increasing frequency. Are you retired yet? Are you still working? What are you killing yourself for? And so on. Each time I thought of fellows like Mick O'Dwyer and Tony Browne and wondered how they coped with enquiring journalists.

Recently I heard of a gentleman who retired some years back and who was regularly asked, "Have you any plans? Do you play the golf?" So he made up his mind that the next time he would be asked, "You retired I hear?" He would get in his reply first and say, "Yeah, and I don't play golf?"

However, since I eventually decided to step down I have been overwhelmed by the good wishes from the people of Thurles. In the early stages I could give the morning going from the top of Liberty Square to the bottom. It is something that will certainly remain with me for the duration of the next stage of my life.

I well remember a comment made by a wellwisher one day and as the conversation continued he said, "Ah sure everybody retires at some stage." At that moment I thought – "A very simple and true statement". When I reflected I thought to myself, "well not everybody retires for the simple reason, unfortunately many do not get that luxurious opportunity". Co-incidentally a day or two later I read in a daily newspaper where some research had shown that 26% of men die before they reach retirement age. A

Incoming Principal, Miriam Butler, makes a presentation on behalf of the staff on retirement night

Retirement cake. The 0-03 bit was tasty but the 5-21 bit stuck in my throat!

sobering thought indeed, and sufficient to remind you – if you didn't already know – how appreciative you should be to have reached that stage of life. I can only humbly thank my Creator for that privilege.

As for the final farewell from the boys and staff of Scoil Ailbhe, I wouldn't even do it justice by saying it was truly memorable. A stage performance of "This is Your Life" by boys representing all classes was both flattering and immensely humorous and entertaining. A whole school rendition of "The Parting Glass" brought the curtain down on both the performance and an enriching and absorbing career.